A Parable a Day

Keeps the Devil at Bay

A Parable a Day

Keeps the Devil at Bay

Wanda Vassallo

lifting up the Light of the world

Wilson NC 27893

Library of Congress Cataloging-in-Publication Data

Vassallo, Wanda
    A parable a day keeps the devil at bay: 101
parables for today / Wanda Vassallo.
        176p.   cm.
        Includes index.
        ISBN 0-915541-36-X : $7.00
        1. Devotional exercises. I. Title.
BV4832.2.V377 1989
242-dc19   89-4140
                                                                CIP

Cover design and text illustrations by Wanda Vassallo

Published by
Star Books, Inc.
408 Pearson Street
Wilson, NC 27893

Telephone (919) 237-1591

ISBN: 0-915541-36-X

Contents

THE PARABLE OF:

INDEXES:

7

To my parents, L. O. and Irene Ballard,
who taught me to love the things of the Lord
at a very early age

THE PARABLE OF
THE BOILED CRAB

The wisdom of the prudent is to understand his way: but the folly of fools is deceit.   Proverbs 14:8

I almost stepped on the armored creature as he scurried down the hall, his pincers raised defiantly, ready to attack my toe or anything else that got in his way.

One of Grandma's crabs had escaped its watery grave. All the rest were calmly and agreeably being boiled to perfection in the scalding water. But the escapee had been overlooked in the bottom of the bucket and had been added to the pot after the water had gotten hot. He crawled out--but quick--hurling himself over the side of the stove. He wasn't about to stay around and get cooked.

The rest of the catch of crabs had been lifted into the pot with tongs when the water was cold. It was placed on the stove, and the water was heated gradually. The unsuspecting crustaceans swam happily around, not realizing that the water was, little by little, getting hotter and hotter. They had no idea what was happening to them. And, before they knew it, they had turned into tasty crabmeat to be made into deviled crab and crabmeat balls.

Our consciences are a lot like those crabs. Something that we simply would not consider doing, involvement that seems reprehensible to us and offends our sense of righteousness, doesn't seem so bad when we're exposed to it gradually. When our consciences become dulled as we take small steps down the wrong path, we find it easier and easier to walk down that path, especially when there are others urging us to go with them.

PRAYER: Dear Lord, guide me this day in Your paths of righteousness. Please, Lord, don't let me miss You. I welcome Your correction when I become enthralled by the enticements of this world. Give me a fresh understanding of the importance of keeping my mind stayed on You.

THE PARABLE OF
THE FLOCK OF GEESE

*Two are better than one; because they have a good reward
for their labor. . . . And if one prevail against him, two
shall withstand him; and a threefold cord is not quickly
broken.* Ecclesiastes 4:9,12

It was a beautiful, clear autumn day with just a touch of
crispness in the air--an ideal day to tromp through the
woods amid the leafy cloaks changing from green to gold
and crimson. It was also an ideal day for the geese to
travel on their annual journey south for the cold months of
winter.

Overhead, they provided a fascinating sight as they
flew in perfect V-formation. How on earth did they keep
their ranks so straight? It looked as though they had an
invisible ruler to keep them in line.

Soon another flock flapped into view . . . and
another . . . then another. The airways were being kept
busy by the graceful winged creatures.

As I watched, an interesting maneuver unfolded.
The goose in the center of the V shifted positions with
another member of the flock, who then became the leader.

With a little research, I discovered that the geese
have a very important reason for flying in the dramatic
V-formation and for changing leaders periodically. The
lead goose takes the brunt of the wind and the elements,
deflecting them from the other geese, and making it much
easier for them to fly on their long journey. No goose
remains in the lead more than a few minutes at a time, because taking that much pressure is exhausting. Or-
nithologists tell us that few geese would ever make it to
their destination, flying alone. In order to reach their goal,
they need each other.

The Christian flock can learn much from the geese.
Certainly we need each other to accomplish our purpose.
We cannot reach a dying world or our own community by
playing the Lone Ranger.

Like the goose, the individual Christian needs to
find and fill his or her place in the Body of Christ. The
geese don't argue about who's going to be the leader or

when. They instinctively know when it's their turn to lead; and when their role is to be a follower, they follow the lead goose.

We may not know these things by instinct, but we can know them through the guidance of the Holy Spirit. If we will let Him, He will order our positions and our labor in the church in perfect harmony--even as the flight of the geese is ordered.

PRAYER: Dear Lord, help me to find and fulfill the place You have ordained for me in Your Body. I know that Christian fellowship and corporate worship provide spiritual strength and safety. Empower me to be supportive of others and to receive the support I need to fulfill Your purpose in my life and in Your church.

THE PARABLE OF
THE MISLEADING SIGNS

And thine ears shall hear a word behind thee, saying, This is the way, walk ye in it, when ye turn to the right hand, and when ye turn to the left. Isaiah 30:21

An afternoon and evening in Boston were hardly enough to get even a taste of the excitement and flair of this historic city. A sunset harbor cruise proved to be an interesting and delightful choice to strike up a quick acquaintance with its rich heritage and edifices.

One of the most dramatic sights was the U.S.S. *Constitution*, or *Old Ironsides*, as it grew to be affectionately called. Its stately masts seemed to reek with history and call you back to another day, another time. Our boat lingered in the bay, waiting for the sun to set--the signal for the firing of a cannon from the deck of the *Constitution*. As the smoke cleared away, we headed back to dock, but the memory of the moment lingered on through the evening.

We decided that we must walk the decks of *Old Ironsides* in the morning before leaving on the next leg of our journey. So we set out on Boston freeways just past rush hour. No problem. We were surprised that getting downtown at that time of day was so easy. Armed with our trusty map, we were soon in the dock area and were seeing signs pointing the way to the U.S.S. *Constitution*. At least we *thought* they were pointing the way. Trying to follow them was a challenge that was not leading to our desired destination.

Suddenly, there it was--the picturesque sailing vessel in all its glory. Now we were on the right track. Then another sign: "U.S.S. *Constitution*, turn right." We almost did--down a one-way street with traffic headed straight toward us. Apparently the city had changed the traffic patterns, but the directions to the ship gave outdated (and dangerous) advice.

We kept trying other streets, studying the map and attempting to go in the direction of the ship. Finally, after several dead ends and wrong turns, we were there. The tour proved to be worth the trouble and the delay. We were enchanted by this priceless piece of our American heritage. But it would have been so much easier if the signs had given the right directions!

There are also many wrong signals in our journey through life--things that would divert our steps from the spiritual path we are trying to walk. How fortunate we are, though, that our heavenly Father will direct us and guide us in all things if we will but ask.

PRAYER: Dear Father, I thank You for Your faithfulness in providing direction and guidance in all my ways. Help me to recognize Your voice and to be mindful of and obedient to Your leading. I praise You for bringing me this far and for Your promise to keep me in the days ahead.

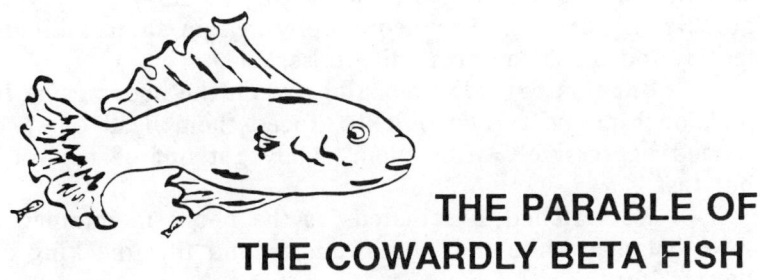

THE PARABLE OF THE COWARDLY BETA FISH

Ye are of God, little children, and have overcome them: because greater is he that is in you, than he that is in the world. 1 John 4:4

Ricky burst into the house breathless and white as a sheet. "What's wrong, son?" I asked.

"Oh, Steve chased me home from school again," he mumbled.

"Well, this is getting to be a habit," I observed. "You know you don't have to let him get by with that."

"But I'm scared of him," Ricky admitted.

"I know, but you don't have to be. He's trying to bluff you. I just know that if you'll stand up to him, he'll leave you alone, and then you can be friends again," I suggested.

As he ate his cookies and milk, deep in thought, he looked serious as only a first-grader can.

I was glad it was Friday. This was a replay of a scene that had happened for the last five days. "Maybe over the weekend," I hoped, "I can think of something that will help him."

The next day the activity in our aquarium, as if on cue, provided the solution.

The children had really enjoyed the antics of the various fish in our underwater community. They decided the graceful movement of the angel fish qualified them as the ballet dancers of the bunch. It was always an exciting event when one of the lady guppies or swords produced offspring. Most fascinating of all were the relationships within the tank.

The largest fish in the tank was the beautifully colored beta fish; yet he let two tiny neons, about one-tenth his size, completely intimidate him. They would nip at him, and he would cower in terror, swimming away as quickly as possible. The neons delighted in their bullying tactics and made the beta's life miserable.

But that Saturday morning, when the neons came to pick on him, he turned quickly, faced them head-on, and started aggressively after them. They got out of his way, but fast.

We watched, fascinated, as the neons maintained a safe distance while the beta swam around like the king of the territory.

"Hey, Ricky, did you see that?" I almost shouted. "That's what I've been talking about. The neons were really cowards once the beta called their bluff."

"Yeah," he squealed, his eyes dancing.

Monday afternoon, Ricky almost swaggered into the house. "How was your walk home from school?" I asked, already knowing the answer.

"Fine," he said, matter-of-factly. "I told Steve to get lost . . . and he did."

The beta and Ricky both learned something very important that Saturday morning. From that day on they were treated with a new respect. Their adversaries knew they were bested.

Too often, when satan attacks us, we act like the beta used to act. We cower and tremble with fright--when actually, with Christ, we are giants in comparison with the limited power of satan.

Once we get on the offensive, stand our ground, and start acting in the authority of Christ, satan will flee--just as quickly as those neons.

PRAYER: Dear Lord, thank You for the power that You have given me in Jesus' name to overcome satan and his works. Help me to stand with might. Give me Your wisdom to know and recognize the tactics and ways of the enemy and to take authority over the powers of darkness.

THE PARABLE OF
THE SHEEP AND THE GOATS

*And he shall set the sheep on his right hand, but the goats
on the left. Then shall the King say unto them on his right
hand, Come, ye blessed of my Father, inherit the kingdom
prepared for you from the foundation of the world. . . .
Then shall he say also unto them on the left hand, Depart
from me, ye cursed, into everlasting fire, prepared for the
devil and his angels.* Matthew 25:33-34, 41

The statement seemed to jump off the page.

I was doing research on the customs and conditions
of Jesus' day for a project I was working on. It was fascinating. The background information was lending a new
depth to what I had learned from studying the New Testament. I found the people I had read about becoming more
three-dimensional as I learned about their daily life and
surroundings.

"Why haven't I done this before?" I was asking
myself as I studied about the occupations of the day. I was
reading about the shepherds when I came across a real
nugget of truth with great spiritual application.

The book said that the shepherds of that day
usually had both sheep and goats in their herds. What
caught my attention was the statement that the shepherd
had to drive the goats, but he could not drive the sheep.
He had to lead them.

I stopped short in my study. I knew there was great
wisdom there, if only I could ferret it out. Slowly it

emerged. "It's no wonder that Jesus spoke often of sheep and goats and called pastors 'shepherds,'" I mused.

Sheep and goats are tremendously different by nature. A shepherd or pastor who insists on driving and goading his flock will attract goats, because sheep will not be driven. But a pastor who leads and provides the right example will be followed by a congregation of healthy, growing sheep.

Which would you rather be--a sheep or a goat? If your pastor must beat you over the head to get you to do what you should be doing, then you're a goat. But if you are eager to follow the shepherd that God has placed over you and to grow up as a Christian, then no doubt your place is in the sheepfold, on the right hand of God.

PRAYER: Dear Lord, I want to be a sheep, not a goat. I thank You for the earthly shepherd You have given me to guide my growth as Your child. I lift up my pastor to You this day, asking a special blessing for his work and in every facet of the life of Your chosen one.

THE PARABLE OF THE VOLCANIC CAKE

But the wisdom that is from above is first pure, then peaceable, gentle, and easy to be intreated, full of mercy and good fruits, without partiality, and without hypocrisy.

James 3:17

Suddenly I smelled something burning. I checked the time. No, the cake wasn't supposed to be done for another twenty minutes. But since it was the only thing cooking, I warily peeked inside the oven. There I saw the strangest sight I had ever seen as a cook. The cake looked like it was erupting. Batter was spewing out over the top of the pan and onto the bottom of the oven. "Mount Vesuvius has nothing on this cake," I thought as I watched a colossal mess developing in the bottom of the oven.

I spent the next half hour cleaning it up and trying to figure out what on earth had happened. I had made that pound cake dozens of times. I could almost throw it together in my sleep: 3 sticks of margarine, 1 box of powdered sugar, 6 eggs, enough flour to fill the powdered-sugar box, 1 tablespoon of vanilla, 1 box of frozen strawberries--a simple recipe.

I tried to recall the mixing process. With two toddlers and their creative ideas sharing the kitchen with me, maybe I had left out an ingredient. "But that wouldn't make the thing overflow that way," I reasoned.

Talk about a mystery! I just couldn't figure it out. I started dinner, still pondering what could have gone wrong. As I reached inside the kitchen cabinet, I discovered the culprit. The flour I had used was self-rising instead of all-purpose. I had asked my husband to pick up some flour at the grocery store on his way home from work, and I hadn't noticed that he had gotten the wrong kind.

I couldn't blame my husband. I hadn't told him to be sure to get all-purpose flour. I surely couldn't blame the flour. After all, it was only doing what it was made to do. If I had been more observant, I wouldn't have been stuck with a ruined dessert and a mess to clean up.

But I also would not have had an excellent example of what happens when we unknowingly mix the wrong ingredients. There are certain principles that work a certain way--regardless of our intent.

Spiritual principles are like that too. Just as surely as the laws of physics, they unerringly bring about positive or negative end results, according to the way they are applied. That's why it's so important to know and understand spiritual principles and how they work, and to be certain that we are using them correctly in our lives.

PRAYER: Lord, give me a greater desire to study Your Word so that I may know and understand spiritual principles. Guard me from error as I try to apply them to my life. Give me Your wisdom as I attempt to glorify You in all I do.

THE PARABLE OF
THE PENNILESS MILLIONAIRE

Lay not up for yourselves treasures upon earth, where moth and rust doth corrupt, and where thieves break through and steal: but lay up for yourselves treasures in heaven, where neither moth nor rust doth corrupt, and where thieves do not break through nor steal.   Matthew 6:19-20

"What was it like during the Depression?" I asked my mother.

"Well, things were pretty grim," she reflected. "Fortunately your father didn't lose his job, but he had to take a drastic salary cut. We couldn't make our house payments, but we managed to keep the interest paid, so we didn't lose our home. It was rough, but we were better off than most. A lot of people of great wealth lost everything they had. Many jumped from tall buildings or found other ways to end their lives. They just couldn't face it."

"Did you know anyone who committed suicide?" I wanted to know.

"No, but we knew a man worth over a million dollars who lost every cent he had," she reminisced.

"What did he do?"

"Well, he was a man of great faith," she recalled. "He had always given generously to the work of the Lord. He had helped support several missionaries in their work overseas for a number of years and had always made liberal offerings to his church. When the great stock-market crash came, he lost everything. Someone said to him, 'Well, I guess you wish now you had all that money you gave to the church and those missionaries.'"

This was really getting interesting. "What did he say?" I asked eagerly.

"Well, he just looked at the other man for a moment and shook his head. Finally, he said, 'Oh, no! You see, that's all I have left.' Then, pointing up toward heaven, he added, 'And it's on deposit.'"

I never knew that penniless millionaire, but he left a lasting legacy in my heart and mind, just as he must have for all who knew him. Fortunately, despite his great earthly wealth, he had learned the secret of true prosperity and security by laying up heavenly treasures. And, through his example and reaction to adversity, he shared that lesson with all who knew him.

PRAYER: Dear Lord, I thank You for the example of the saints who have gone before me. Help me always to be mindful of the importance of investing my time and money in eternal treasures rather than in temporal trifles. Increase my desire to build my bank account in heaven.

THE PARABLE OF THE UNEXPLAINED DESERT

The grass withereth, the flower fadeth: but the word of our God shall stand for ever. Isaiah 40:8

As we looked out over the vast stretches of sand sparkling in the early morning sun, it was hard to imagine that once this had been a farm supporting crops and animals. The old barn still stands and contains some of the original tools and artifacts reclaimed from the dunes that now cover about four hundred acres of land. Other farm buildings are completely buried by the tons of sand which, in some spots, stand seventy feet high.

This is the Desert of Maine, located only a few miles from the Atlantic Ocean. No one knows what caused the fertile farmland to turn into a vast desert. Geologists have been unable to explain the strange phenomenon, but they predict that in time it will once again revert back to its original soil.

The change began some eighty-five years ago, when the owner noticed that, where the cows had pulled up tufts of grass, sand had begun to appear. He looked at the small sandy patch of ground, wondered about it, and then dismissed it from his mind. But soon the patch began to grow . . . and grow . . . and grow. Finally, several years later, he had to abandon his occupation there. The sand had taken over. It was impossible to grow crops.

Another inexplicable thing about this strange desert is that trees, some covered by forty or fifty feet of sand, continue to grow and thrive. How do their roots get enough moisture? It's a mystery, but they continue to live and provide a jarring contrast to the starkness of the light-colored sand.

A century ago, no one would have dreamed that some day there would be a desert in the state of Maine. As we walked across the warm sand, I thought of the ever-changing pattern of our lives.

Many times we don't understand the events and circumstances that surround us. We ask why, and seem to get no response. We seem to want to cling to the familiar, but we really cannot count on anything remaining the same--with a notable exception. Neither God nor the things of God ever change. His Word is just as true today as the day it was written . . . and it always will be. He's the one thing we can count on.

PRAYER: Dear Lord, thank You that, with the changing sands of time, relationships, and circumstances, You are always the same. You are always there when I need You. You have never failed me, and I know that You never will. In return, I want to be faithful to You in every facet of my life. Please help me to increase in faithfulness.

THE PARABLE OF
THE SCHOOL-BOARD MEETING

For we must all appear before the judgment seat of Christ; that every one may receive the things done in his body, according to that he hath done, whether it be good or bad.
2 Corinthians 5:10

How could I have forgotten? It was only fifteen minutes until the Board of Education meeting was to begin, and I didn't have the resolutions of recognition ready to be presented to those who had been invited to be commended by the school board.

A part of my job was to write the resolutions, have them entered on the agenda for approval by the board, invite the recipients to the meeting, and have the resolutions typed on parchment paper, signed by the president and superintendent, and topped with the official, embossed school-district seal. They were to be at the board president's place at the beginning of the meeting.

That particular day I had gone out to lunch with some fellow staff members and leisurely enjoyed a respite from the day's work.

But that relaxed attitude had swiftly turned to panic as I realized the predicament I was in. My secretary was at lunch. I hastily ran downstairs to another secretary who had graciously stayed after working hours several times in the past to help me meet a deadline. I hurriedly explained my dilemma. Without blinking an eye, she said, "Sorry. I'm on my way to lunch," as she brushed past me.

I raced down the hall to my boss's secretary, checking the time as I went. She was very gracious and started typing away. "Surely the meeting will start late," I thought. "It usually does." A quick trip to the auditorium denied that hope. The meeting was already in session. As I headed back down the hall, I thought, "Well, the superintendent usually makes a rather long opening report." I then discovered that I had not given the secretary the first resolution on the agenda to type.

The next few minutes seemed like an eternity as I shuttled documents up and down the hall and climbed over chairs to try to get signatures. When I finally returned with the first resolution to be presented, I learned that it had already been called for. The person being honored came forward, but there was no resolution. I was embarrassed almost to tears. I wanted to crawl under my seat as the person was called forward a second time with the pointed explanation that "now at last we have the resolution ready for you."

Even though I was not reprimanded and my boss laughed it off, I felt terrible. My lack of attention had marred what should have been a very special moment. I couldn't shake off the humiliation I felt. But in the back of my mind, I sensed that there was something of more significance than a botched-up presentation.

For several weeks I believed that the Lord had been directing me to start a prayer-and-share group at work. I had all sorts of "reasons" why that wouldn't be possible: "I don't know how." "I would be glad to be supportive of someone else starting one, but I just couldn't do that myself." "I would have to get permission." My excuses went on and on.

Over the weekend, the Lord showed me the connection. He spoke to me not in the usual still, small voice, but in what seemed an amplified shout. "If you think you were embarrassed at the school board meeting, just wait until you stand before the judgment seat if you have not been obedient to My direction." Suddenly "Daddy" became "The Father," and I instantly understood the high priority and value He places on the obedience of His children.

The next week I got permission to organize a prayer group, and sent out a note to several people I thought might be interested. The Prayer and Share Group began meeting weekly and touched many lives during the two-and-a-half years of its existence.

PRAYER: Dear Lord, I thank You for sending me to obedience school and for impressing on me the importance of being ready and willing to do Your bidding. Place a greater desire in my heart to do the things You would have me do, knowing that Your way is far superior to mine. I want my will for my life to coincide perfectly with Your will as I walk day by day.

THE PARABLE OF
THE DESTRUCTIVE MOTHS

For such are false apostles, deceitful workers, transforming themselves into the apostles of Christ. And no marvel; for satan himself is transformed into an angel of light.
2 Corinthians 11:13-14

The light-colored "lint" did not disappear as I tried to pluck it from my navy-blue wool skirt. A closer look revealed the reason. There was a tiny hole, and my beige-colored slip was shining brightly through. Obviously a moth had found its way to my closet. I pulled my sweater down lower over my skirt, hoping no one else would notice.

Over the next few weeks, I was horrified to find that several other garments containing wool had been visited by the destructive pests. There was always one small hole per dress or skirt. "At least they could have been considerate enough to eat all of one instead of riddling several," I complained to myself. And they seemed to pick some of my favorites to munch on.

Fortunately, by carefully matching the thread and investing considerable time and patience, I was able to execute a facsimile of re-weaving that hid the telltale holes. But every time I take out another dress, sweater, or skirt containing wool, I look closely to see if it has fallen prey to the spoilers.

It's difficult to believe that anything so graceful and beautiful can be so destructive. Moths have much in common with the butterfly, my favorite creature. Together, they form one insect order. The stages in their development are the same: from egg to caterpillar to cocoon to adult. And, of course, they both soar through the air on their artistically colored wings.

An interesting difference between them is that butterflies are usually out during daylight hours, while moths come out at dusk or at night. Moths never fly around lights. In fact, if a light is turned on, moths will fly away from it. But the most significant difference--at least as far as my wardrobe is concerned--is that butterflies don't ruin clothing.

The wiles of satan often come in pleasant, beautiful outward appearances--just as the moth does. And, like the moth, they cannot stand the light. Unless we are on guard, things that seem innocent and even intriguing can be very destructive once they gain entry into the closets of our lives.

PRAYER: I thank You that You are my Shepherd and that I can follow, without fear, wherever You lead me, knowing that I will be safe from satan's strategies of destruction. Please keep me from being deceived by the tinsel and intrigue of worldly attractions. Give me acute power of discernment, so that I will instantly know the difference between the good and the counterfeit.

THE PARABLE OF
THE MISSED OPPORTUNITY

Say not ye, There are yet four months, and then cometh harvest? behold, I say unto you, Lift up your eyes, and look on the fields; for they are white already to harvest.

John 4:35

"Miss Alexander asked me today if I wanted to be in a play," I told my mother.

"How nice!" she said enthusiastically.

"But I told her I didn't want to do it," I added quickly.

"Why not?" she asked, disappointment in her voice.

"I was afraid I'd get scared," I explained.

"But that was really an honor that she asked you, and I know you would do well," she said, looking me straight in the eye. "Besides, Miss Alexander wouldn't have asked you if she wasn't sure you could do it. Wanda, you should always take advantage of opportunities that are presented to you. That's the way you grow and learn. Besides, if you turn people down, they may not give you a chance the next time."

Now I started to feel very bad about my refusal. It really would be fun to be in the school play and wear a costume and everything. "Oh, why did I say no?" I thought miserably.

24

"Mother, do you think if I told Miss Alexander tomorrow I'd like to be in it, she'd let me?" I asked hopefully.

"I don't know," she answered, "but it wouldn't hurt to ask."

I didn't sleep well that night, worrying about how I would ask Miss Alexander and what she would say. The night seemed unending, as time can for a seven-year-old.

The next morning I found my teacher in her room before classes began. "Uh . . . Miss Alexander . . . uh . . . I've been thinking about it and I really would like to do that part in the play," I managed to get out shyly.

"Wanda, I'm sorry, but I gave out all the parts yesterday," she said sympathetically. "But I tell you what: you can be the understudy, and then if anyone has to drop out, you can play the part."

I left disappointed, but at least I still *might* be in the play.

I memorized every part. In fact, I could recite the whole play from beginning to end. Whenever anyone was absent, I would play their part in rehearsal. Secretly, I wished someone would get sick so I could take their place. But the evening of the performance, they were all there. I sat in the audience, mentally reciting every part with the actors. But *they* got the applause.

I never forgot that experience. The next time I was asked to do something special at school, I had my "yes" ready well in advance.

I want to be that way in God's kingdom too--always ready to walk through any door He opens for me and to do the work He has for my hands to do. That's the way I learn and grow. And I know He won't ask me to do something unless He is sure I can do it--with His help. I don't want to be an understudy. I want to play the part He has selected for me.

PRAYER: Lord, I thank You for each opportunity You have given me in the past to serve You. Help me to recognize quickly when You are opening a door of service for me and to be ready to respond at once and without reservation. I want to have my "yes" ready immediately, regardless of the task You give me to do.

THE PARABLE OF THE BABY DUCKLING

In all things shewing thyself a pattern of good works . . .
Titus 2:7

Cici struggled out of the water and lay on the bank, looking completely exhausted and pitifully bedraggled. She had almost drowned.

We had tried to coax her into swimming a couple of times before, and she would have no part in it. This time, seeing her mother and siblings gliding effortlessly near the bank, my son decided to toss her out near them. After all, ducks are born knowing how to swim, aren't they?

We finally figured out her problem. It wasn't that she couldn't swim. She didn't know that she was a duck and that she was *supposed* to swim.

Cici's mother had been scared off her nest by the roar of the lawn mower one Saturday evening just as her babies were hatching. I kept looking out at her nest in the hollow of a willow by the lake in our backyard. No mama duck. Finally, about midnight, I went out and placed the newly hatched ducklings and the one remaining egg in a box and brought them into the kitchen. I was afraid a snake or raccoon might have them for a midnight snack.

Early the next morning, there was the mother duck, pacing frantically back and forth on the bank looking for her babies. I took the fluffy little peepers out to her and witnessed a happy reunion. But I kept the egg in the box. By this time, the egg was cracked, and a tiny webbed foot was emerging.

A few hours later Cici was out of the egg, waddling around. I scooped her up and took her to the bank. Her mother and the other ducklings greeted her excitedly. She immediately ran away from them, back to me. When I tried to leave, she absolutely panicked and ran frantically after me as fast as her little legs would carry her. She was so pitiful that I ended up taking her back inside with me.

Later, we learned about imprinting. Ducks think the first moving creature they see is their mother. As far as Cici was concerned, I was her mother, and she was a human being . . . not a duck. Any time she was out of her box, she followed me around or rode on my shoulder. She wanted to be where I was and do what I did. I was her example.

All of us are examples to other people . . . whether or not we realize it or want to be. There are those who are looking at us as examples of what a Christian should be and do. They are patterning their lives after ours, just as Cici patterned after me. My experience with Cici prompts a searching question: Is my life a worthy example of Jesus' love and power?

PRAYER: Dear Lord, make me ever mindful that, as a Christian, I am Your representative wherever I go. Whether I am driving, shopping, playing, worshiping You, or working in the marketplace, there are those who are observing not only my words and actions, but also my attitudes. Help me this day, by Your grace and Your power, to be Your worthy representative.

THE PARABLE OF CICI'S LOVE

Be kindly affectioned one to another with brotherly love; in honour preferring one another. Romans 12:10

It looked like Cici would never have a mate. After all, she thought I was her mother and that she was a girl, not a duck.

After she outgrew the box in our kitchen, my son built her a little pen and put it on the back porch. We were afraid to let her out, for fear she would wander through the small opening between the fence and the gate. As unstreetwise as she was, we feared for her safety if she ventured outside our backyard.

But after she grew too large to squeeze through the gate, we allowed her to wander freely in the fenced yard. One day, I noticed a very beautiful duck standing on the other side of the fence. Cici was in the yard, standing as close to him as possible, as if they were enjoying a conversation. After that, it was not at all unusual to see the handsome drake hovering by the gate. Cici was being courted!

One day Cici flew over the fence and left with him. But every so often, she would return with her mate. He would stand outside the gate and wait for her while she came into the yard and visited with her "mother."

You see, it took love to convince Cici that she really was a duck, and to entice her into living the life she was created to live.

The same thing is true with people. God's love, flowing through us to others, can change past conceptions and habits, and help others to understand and become what God created them to be.

PRAYER: Lord, help me to become a conduit of Your love to others. I ask for Your pure, unconditional love for each person I come in contact with this day. Let me see each individual not with my limited human vision but through Your eyes, that I may envision the person You have created that one to be. And give me the privilege of helping others to see and fulfill that vision in their lives.

THE PARABLE OF
THE EXQUISITE COLORS

The counsel of the Lord standeth for ever, the thoughts of his heart to all generations.   Psalms 33:11

We stood in awe in the great cathedral at Reims, France, marveling at the magnificent beauty of the stained-glass windows.

Over the past few weeks in Europe, we had visited many cathedrals and had gazed in wonder at the intricate craftsmanship of the carvings and stained-glass windows. We realized that these physical objects of beauty had been left as a legacy of love by the thousands of artists who devoted their entire lives to making the house of God a place of beauty.

But these windows were different! The depth and richness of the colors were beyond description--unmatched by any other we had seen. The blue was so dazzling that it made me feel as if I had seen something secret, almost too sacred for the human eye.

Our guide explained sadly that the process used in making this uniquely vibrant stained glass was a lost art. The windows were the workmanship of a family of artists who passed the art of producing those exquisite colors down from one generation to another. The secret died with the last of the family. Many have tried since that time to re-discover the recipe, but all have failed.

No one knows why the formula was lost. We can only guess. Perhaps its worth was not realized by those who came after. Could it be that the directions were scrawled on a scrap of old paper, soiled from constant handling and wear? Perhaps a cleaning woman one day threw it away, not having any idea of its value. Or maybe a younger craftsman decided he could improve on the process by coming up with a more modern, less expensive way, rather than spending countless hours doing the same old thing.

In today's society, no doubt, the latter would be the case. We place so much emphasis on being modern, on finding new and better ways, on being up-to-the minute and doing the "in thing," that it's sometimes difficult to believe that a book written centuries ago could possibly contain all we need to know about leading a fulfilling, satisfying, joy-filled life today.

And yet the words of the Bible are just as true today as the day they were written. Following its precepts brings to our lives the same clarity and beauty that those inspired artists of old brought to the stained-glass windows of the Reims Cathedral. And that beauty will endure not only all our days on earth but forever and ever.

PRAYER: Dear Lord, I thank You for Your word that shows me how to make my life beautiful in Your sight and also in my experience. I ask that You give me a greater desire to study the Bible, and that You increase my understanding of what You are saying to me today.

THE PARABLE OF
THE LIGHTNING BUGS

Ye are the light of the world. A city that is set on a hill cannot be hid.   Matthew 5:14

The night was darker than usual. As we sat on the back porch, we were charmed by the cheerful sparks of the lightning bugs. This year, there were more than usual.

The scene took me back many years to a favorite childhood memory. My father and I had this special little game for a summer evening. I would go out and catch as many lightning bugs as I could find and put them in a jar with air holes in the lid. Just the two of us would then go into the living room, turn out the lights, and watch the little lovelies as they shone their tiny lights in the darkness.

It was always a special time--a time of precious fellowship for a father and his only daughter . . . a time set aside for each other and a time of sharing rare moments. I was always amazed at the amount of light these tiny creatures generated. It was a fascinating experience.

As we sat on the porch, I was once again amazed. Even though most of the lightning bugs were some distance from us, their light was as clear and as attention-getting as if they had been within arm's reach.

"As Christians, how much we can learn from those little bugs," I mused. "Even the least of us has so much to offer. We can shine the light of Christ in a dingy, dreary world. No one can help but notice that light, however small, in the darkness. And it can make a real difference in the lives of others."

PRAYER: Dear Lord, I want to light the path for others. Please show me how. Give me Your words and Your wisdom, that I may encourage Your children. Help me to be a reflection of Your love and Your ways so that others may walk on an illumined pathway.

THE PARABLE OF
THE MISSING SPEECH NOTES

We then, as workers together with him, beseech you also that ye receive not the grace of God in vain. . . . Giving no offence in any thing, that the ministry be not blamed.

2 Corinthians 6:1,3

Panic overtook me. Here I was, moments before I was to be introduced, and the first of my note cards had disappeared. I hastily checked through the small stack, hoping that, somehow, I had gotten the cards out of order and that I would find the missing note card at the bottom. No, it just wasn't there.

Quickly I rummaged through my music, thinking that the card might have gotten stuck between some of the pages. Another disappointment! It was nowhere to be found.

By this time the program chairman was well into the introduction. Frantically I tried to recall the words of the lyric with which I would open my program entitled "America's Story in Folk Music."

My twelve-year-old son was all ready. He was my sound engineer and would play, on cue, recordings of about a dozen pieces as background music. He had a complete copy of the script, with exact cues carefully marked. The forty-five-minute program included folk tales, sayings and explanations, in connection with the eight basic types of folk music I would sing and play. It was a rather complicated presentation--not the type that lent itself to ad-libbing.

I had unwisely laid my notes and music on top of the piano when I came in and started chatting with people. Apparently someone in the group had thought the cards were some kind of handout and had taken the top one. Briefly I considered asking the group who had the card, but I immediately decided that would be too embarrassing for everyone concerned and would get the program off to a disastrous start. Instead, I gritted my teeth into what I hoped was a confident-looking smile and hoped for the best.

I began with as much aplomb as possible considering my sweaty palms and shaking knees. Rick was studiously looking down at the script, ready to start the tape recorder when I gave the cue. After a couple of sentences, he started searching through his script and then looked at me with a very puzzled expression on his face. This definitely was not the way we had rehearsed it. The words weren't matching up. Finally, I gave him a hand cue to start the first song.

Somehow I managed to stumble through the first part of the program, although I'm sure it lacked the flavor and punch it should have had. What a relief when I reached the second segment of the script!

After finishing my presentation, I laid my music and notes on the piano while refreshments were being served. When I went back to retrieve them, there was the first note card, returned to its proper place on top of the stack. I never did learn who had the card, but I did learn a good rule that I've followed ever since: Hold on to your notes for dear life if you're going to make a speech.

I also learned, firsthand, how a seemingly innocent action can have a negative impact or influence on another person. The success of my presentation was not a matter of life or death, but what I say and do *can* be a matter of life or death spiritually for someone who is watching me as a Christian example.

PRAYER: Dear Lord, help me to be ever mindful of the impact of my words and actions on others. Help me to be an example of Christian love by the testimony of my lips and life, giving no occasion of offense to any man or woman, boy or girl.

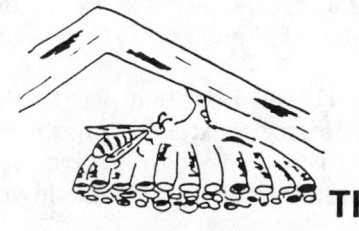

THE PARABLE OF THE YELLOW JACKETS

When the unclean spirit is gone out of a man, he walketh through dry places, seeking rest; and finding none, he saith, I will return unto my house whence I came out. And when he cometh, he findeth it swept and garnished. Then goeth he, and taketh to him seven other spirits more wicked than himself; and they enter in, and dwell there: and the last state of that man is worse than the first. Luke 11:24-26

Yellow jackets are persistent creatures. I found that out the hard way when I decided to remove their nest from the eaves of the house near the front porch.

Getting them away from the nest so I could knock it down was no easy task. Finally, after making several spray attacks and hurried retreats, I was able to sever their intricate structure from the wood.

I felt good about my brave deed and was relieved to be rid of the well-armed insects. But a few days later I noticed a yellow jacket flitting around the area and discovered that they had made great progress in rebuilding their apartment complex in exactly the same spot.

Out came the spray and the broom again, as I once more gathered up the courage to try to oust the intruders from their nest. I ran even faster to get away from their angry aerial attacks. At last, however, my mission was accomplished and the paperish house was smashed on the ground.

Soon, though, they were right back once more, working feverishly in the same place. For a while I wasn't sure who was going to win. They would build it back; I would knock it down, and on and on. But finally, they did not return.

Satan operates exactly the same way as those yellow jackets. He tries to find a void place, a weakness in our lives where he can gain a foothold. He will harass us in that area until we rise up under the power of God and chase him away.

We're so relieved to be rid of him that we don't always notice he has come back to try to attach himself in exactly the same spot in our lives. He doesn't give up easily. He will keep coming back, attempting to wear down our resistance.

But eventually--as we consistently stand against him--he decides he can't lick us and goes his way.

PRAYER: Dear Lord, I thank You for the strength You provide in areas of my weakness. Give me the insight to recognize and the determination to destroy any strongholds that satan has managed to establish in my life. And once they are gone, help me to keep the enemy from regaining that ground.

THE PARABLE OF
THE HIGH DIVING BOARD

For therein is the righteousness of God revealed from faith to faith: as it is written, The just shall live by faith.
Romans 1:17

All summer, I had been trying to get up nerve enough to climb up on the high diving board. I had secretly envied all my brave friends who would race up to the top and dive gracefully off time after time. It looked like such fun.

Well, I had made up mind. Today was going to be the day. I didn't plan to dive. I knew that just jumping feet first would be adventure enough--or too much--for my first attempt. I dived confidently off the low board several times and swam out to the island and back in preparation for the gigantic feat.

Finally I decided, "This is it." I had checked out the ladder. No one was anywhere near. "I can always climb back down if it's too scary," I reasoned, as any sensible thirteen-year-old would.

Trying to look nonchalant, I placed my foot on the first metal rung. Its intense heat from the blistery Texas sun sped me on my way to the top. Before I knew what was happening, I had scaled the ladder and was walking gingerly to the edge of the diving board.

Only then did I allow myself to look down at the water, which appeared to be at least a mile below. I was scared out of my wits, frozen in horror. Just as I decided to climb back down, I heard a voice behind me shouting, "Hurry up!"

A quick glance back revealed several heads at various heights on the ladder, all looking up at me. Where had they come from?

Soon the one voice was joined by several others. "Go on and jump!" "Get out of the way!"

I was panic-stricken at the thought of jumping-- but I really had no choice. I hastily put my hand over my nose and leaped reluctantly off the end of the board.

To my amazement, I lived through it and almost enjoyed the sensation of falling through the air. I even jumped two more times that afternoon and soon decided it was fun. But I might never have learned that if I hadn't been more or less forced into trying it.

There are times in our lives when we find ourselves in a position of having to rely on God. We simply have no other resource. It is then that we learn a lesson in faith. Then, as we grow from faith to faith, we begin to enjoy the assurance of His faithfulness in every situation. Instead of being *forced* to use our faith, we can exercise it voluntarily, confident of His presence and His power to work in all things for good.

PRAYER: Dear Lord, I thank You for the measure of faith You have given me. Help me to be diligent in exercising it, so that my spiritual muscles will be well developed. When my faith gets flabby, please bring to my mind the many instances of Your faithfulness, so that I may step out in faith to do mighty things in Your name.

THE PARABLE OF
THE NAME-DROPPER

But the very hairs of your head are all numbered. Fear ye not, therefore, ye are of more value than many sparrows.
                                            Matthew 10:30-31

"This is Wanda Vassallo. I'm calling for the superintendent of the Dallas schools."

As speechwriter for the superintendent of schools, I often had to telephone important people for information about his speaking engagements. I had learned through experience that those words--"calling for the superintendent" --got me through immediately to Dallas' most influential citizens. Mentioning his name was also invaluable when I needed to talk with a principal or a top administrator.

If I forgot to drop my boss's name, most secretaries politely refused to put my call through. They didn't know who Wanda Vassallo was and couldn't care less--but no one was ever too busy to talk to me when I was "calling for the superintendent." I found that name-dropping came in very handy indeed and made my job a lot easier.

But I don't need to be a name-dropper when I want to talk with God. I don't have to say I'm calling for my pastor in order to get through to Him. In fact, I don't even have to give my name. He knows my voice. He always has an open line, and He doesn't put me on hold. He's never too busy or too tired to talk with me, regardless of the hour.

PRAYER: Lord, I thank You that You are never too busy to talk to me. It is hard to believe (but I know it's true) that You, the God of the whole universe, not only know my name and everything about me, but that You love me without reservation. Thank You for Your faithfulness. Please help me to be faithful in return.

THE PARABLE OF
THE UNWELCOME VISITOR

Then shall they also answer him, saying, Lord, when saw we thee an hungred or athirst, or a stranger, or naked, or sick, or in prison, and did not minister unto thee? Then shall he answer them, saying, Verily I say unto you, Inasmuch as ye did it not to one of the least of these, ye did it not to me. Matthew 25:44-45

Huge teardrops cascaded down her cheeks, threatening to flood the papers on my desk. Quickly I handed her a Kleenex. I sure didn't want her tears to mess up the letter-perfect first page of the church newsletter I was working on.

"This is the worst thing that ever happened to me," she sobbed. "Here I've given the school district the best twenty years of my life, and what do I get in return?"

Sue was one of 200-some victims of cutbacks on the central staff, leaving them without jobs for the coming school year. I had always liked her, even though she was only an acquaintance. I was surprised that she was sharing her innermost feelings with me . . . and, I must admit, more than a little irritated.

After all, I had a deadline to meet. I had rushed around like a maniac to get to my office by 7 A.M. so I would have a whole hour to work on the newsletter before starting my day's work. I simply did not have time to talk to Sue . . . or anyone else. "If only I had closed that door so she wouldn't know I was here," I thought.

The conversation dragged on and on. Finally, after what seemed like an eternity, she turned to leave. "I really appreciate your talking with me," she said with sincerity. "I needed a sympathetic ear. What you said really helped."

"That's good. I know things will turn out all right for you," I murmured. As soon as she turned the corner, I raced to the door, closed it quickly, and locked it. No one else was going to usurp my precious moments of time. After all, I had to get this newsletter done for the Lord.

My fingers were flying over the typewriter keys, trying to make up for lost time, when suddenly it hit me! Sue's visit was actually in answer to a prayer I had spoken only a few minutes earlier as I drove to work. "O Lord, please let me be a blessing to someone today," I had prayed.

My fingers froze in mid-air. I had had the perfect opportunity to be a real blessing to Sue. And how had I responded? With irritation and impatience when she dared to infringe on my precious time with her problems.

I wanted to run after her, to bring her back, to ask her forgiveness, to tell her of God's love and concern for what she was going through, to share with her some of the mighty things He has done in my life through what seemed like severe trials at the time. I hurried out into the hall. But it was too late. She had disappeared.

I don't know what happened to Sue. But I do know what happened to me as a result of that early-morning meeting. I learned to let God decide how I can best use my time for Him, and to expect Him to answer my prayers in unexpected and, sometimes, inconvenient ways.

PRAYER: Dear Lord, please forgive me for the times when You have sent one of Your children my way and I have responded with impatience and irritation rather than with love and encouragement. Help me always to be sensitive to the opportunities You bring me to reach out to others in Your name.

THE PARABLE OF
THE POTS OF IVY

Death and life are in the power of the tongue: and they that love it shall eat the fruit thereof.   Proverbs 18:21

The third-grade class had been studying about plants. Gradually the idea developed for a scientific experiment in plant-growing.

The children, with the guidance of their teacher, decided to find out what effect their attitude and the way they treated plants would have on their growth. They chose ivy plants as the subject of their experiment. Three plants, as nearly identical as possible, were selected and purchased to become residents of the classroom.

They were conscientiously given the same physical care--identical amounts of light, water, and nutrients. One factor, however, was different, and that was their "emotional" treatment.

One ivy had soothing music played for it. The second plant was told by the children in endearing tones, each time they entered and left the classroom, how beautiful it was and how much they loved it. But the third one had only insults hurled at it: "You're the ugliest thing I've ever seen." "I hope you drop dead!" "I hate you!" Those were the kinds of messages the poor little plant had shouted at it day after day.

The results were amazing, even to those who had expected a difference. The ivy that heard music grew long runners, but not very many leaves. The admired and complimented plant thrived, growing profuse and luxuriantly beautiful foliage. And the verbally abused plant? Well, it just withered up and died.

If that's the result with plants, just think how much of an impact kind, encouraging, loving words or critical, rejecting, demeaning words have on people! What we say can inspire others to grow, bloom, and become all that God created them to be. Or we can discourage them so that they dry up and die on the vine.

Scripture tells us, "Death and life are in the power of the tongue" (Proverbs 18:21). The children's experiment proves the truth of Solomon's statement.

PRAYER: Lord, help me to realize the impact of my words on the lives of others. When I am tempted to respond with a sharp tongue or a cutting statement to show that I am clever, stop me short and remind me of how I would feel if I were the recipient of what I am poised to say. Assist me in shaping words of edification, encouragement, and hope in every situation.

THE PARABLE OF THE HUNGRY FROG

And Jesus said unto him, No man having put his hand to the plough, and looking back, is fit for the kingdom of God.
Luke 9:62

I trotted along behind my cousin, trying with all my might not to lag behind. His long-legged gait challenged my small feet, trained only to walk on concrete sidewalks. We were on our way to the tank, quite an adventure for a city girl.

"Watch that snake, Wanda," he shouted back over his shoulder. I bounded to catch up with him. I had never seen a snake, except in a cage at the zoo, at that close range, and I had no intention of getting better acquainted with it.

My cousin laughed at my haste in getting away from the slithery creature. "Just wait till we get to the tank," he chortled. "That's where they really hang out."

Oh, great! I thought, with an overwhelming desire to bolt back to the safety of the sturdy old farmhouse. I was really getting scared . . . but I wasn't about to let him know it.

"But they won't bother you," he said reassuringly. "They're just water snakes, and they're scareder of you than you are of them."

The tank proved to be a fascinating place. The quietness, pierced only by the occasional croak of a bullfrog and the song of a bobwhite, amazed me. The emerald trees, which spread their arms over delicate buttercups nodding in the gentle spring breeze, were a sight to behold.

But the thing that riveted my attention was a huge bullfrog sitting silently on a stump by the water. He was so still, he almost appeared to be a statue. He stared, his glance unwavering. Then, in the twinkling of an eye, his long tongue shot out, trapping an unsuspecting fly. He then sat back, enjoying his catch. He repeated his act several times, until he had eaten his fill.

My cousin explained that the frog is equipped with a sticky substance on his tongue that bonds to any insect it contacts, making it impossible for the hapless victim to get away.

As Christians, we can learn from that frog. We too are equipped--with protective armor and with every weapon we need to lead a victorious life.

Once the frog had decided to catch a certain insect, he never wavered from his intention. He kept his eye on the goal. It didn't matter what was going on around him. He didn't care what the snakes were doing, or the other frogs. He had a made-up mind--to catch that fly.

We too need to make up our minds--to follow Christ, regardless of circumstances or what others might be doing.

PRAYER: Lord, help me to keep my eyes on You and not be distracted by the enticements the world has to offer. I pray this day for a made-up mind to follow You and to look to You in every area of living, so that I may accomplish the goals You have set for me.

THE PARABLE OF
THE BOUNTIFUL ESCROW ACCOUNT

But my God shall supply all your need according to his riches in glory by Christ Jesus.   Philippians 4:19

We had decided to go to Maine. We felt we just couldn't let our daughter strike out alone in her beat-up station wagon that had seen more than 100,000 miles of strenuous duty. She had to take her harp and had no choice but to drive her rickety vehicle.

I found the idea of the trip exciting. I had never been to the New England states and had heard many times of their charm and beauty. Our son, who had not had a vacation in more than two years, offered to let us drive his new van, caravan-style behind his sister. He then would fly to Portland, Maine, and join us for ten days of sightseeing on the way home. We would come back through Boston, Cape Cod, and New York City, and see several other places we had never been before. It really sounded stimulating and interesting.

But as I started checking the prices of motels in some of the places we would be staying, I realized that this was going to be an expensive trip! I hated to take the money out of savings, but there seemed to be no other way.

Then I remembered two things: the property-tax refund we had applied for for the previous year, and something I had heard in a seminar.

"You really ought to check your escrow account on your home loan," the speaker had said. "Often there's a lot more money in your account than is needed to pay your insurance and taxes."

A couple of phone calls revealed that the property-tax refund had been sent to our loan company and placed in our escrow account. The balance showed a surplus of more than $2,000!

"I'd take it all out if I were you," the teller told my husband. "It's not drawing any interest or anything. Would you like to open a savings account with it?"

"No," he replied. "I think we're supposed to use that money for another purpose."

42

The $2,000 was more than enough for the trip. And it had been there all the time, just waiting for us.

That's the way it is with God's provision and His love. It's there for us all the time, whenever we need it. And He's more than enough in every situation.

PRAYER: Dear Lord, thank You for Your constant and unfathomable love and provision. I never cease to be amazed at the endless creative ways in which You turn impossibilities into realities in my life. Help me to rest in You, knowing that You are Jehovah-Jireh, my provider.

THE PARABLE OF THE CAGEY CHIPMUNK

Behold, I stand at the door, and knock: if any man hear my voice, and open the door, I will come in to him, and will sup with him, and he with me. Revelation 3:20

My son and I were hiking on a trail in Acadia National Park when we ran across a delightfully whimsical chipmunk that looked as if he had just hopped out of a Walt Disney movie.

He stopped in mid-run, sat up on his hind legs, and looked quizzically our way, his head tilted fetchingly to one side. What a picture! We reached for our cameras to try to capture this appealing little creature. Just as I was getting ready to snap the shutter and Rick to begin videotaping, the chipmunk darted off.

We shared our disappointment in not getting his picture, and turned our attention to other fascinating facets of our exquisite surroundings--the dainty ferns, different types of mosses, beautiful trees, rocks, and pine cones. Then, all of a sudden, there the chipmunk was again, dashing around among the pine needles. He stopped once more, carefully scrutinizing us as though trying to decide if we were friends or foes.

We stood like statues as he tentatively came closer to us. We could actually hear his tiny feet brushing the leaves in the sheer silence of the forest. Once again, up went our cameras. If only . . . but then he suddenly veered off and out of sight.

Then as we were turning to go in a different direction, he just as suddenly appeared, coming even closer this time and stopping upright as though posing for us. Then he was off again.

For at least five minutes, he repeated his antics. He would run away and then, just when we thought he was gone for good, he would pop up. Rick finally got some interesting footage of his capers before he disappeared for good.

There seemed to be something about us that kept attracting the chipmunk to us. But we were much more eager to be with him than he was to be with us. Otherwise, he would not have kept running away.

I wonder how many times God must feel somewhat as we did that day--always eager and ready to commune with us. How many times do we get closer to Him--only to turn aside and go our own way? He waits patiently, wanting to have fellowship with His children.

PRAYER: Dear Lord, I thank You that You are always ready to visit with me--even when I seem to be preoccupied with earthly things. Don't let me take Your presence for granted. Help me to draw closer and stay closer to You as I walk this earthly path.

THE PARABLE OF
THE UNFRUITFUL TOMATO PLANTS

Ye have not chosen me, but I have chosen you, and ordained you, that ye should go and bring forth fruit, and that your fruit should remain: that whatsoever ye shall ask of the Father in my name, he may give it you. John 15:16

"How did he know I was growing tomatoes?" I asked my husband.

I had never seen such a large, brightly colored worm in my life. He was a shocking chartreuse and looked like something Walt Disney might have dreamed up for one of his animated cartoons. If he had been any larger, I probably would have run the other way.

I bent down and inspected the fledgling, healthy-looking plants. Sure enough, the tomato worm had enjoyed a hearty last meal at their expense before his untimely death.

A few weeks later, I got excited. The tomato plants had a number of blossoms. We were going to be eating a lot of home-grown tomatoes. I could hardly wait. But the next day brought disappointment. Several blossoms were missing. Only a tiny stem remained, looking as though it had been chopped off with a knife. Cutworms! I dusted the plants to get rid of those destructive pests.

I waited and waited . . . but still no juicy tomatoes.

I asked a friend who teaches horticulture what I was doing wrong. "Well, you might be using the wrong fertilizer," he observed. "There are three numbers you have to look at. The first number determines the greenness and growth of the vines and leaves. The second one has to be just right in order for the fruit to set. The third number determines the root growth. And you have to be sure the roots are protected. If you water them in the late evening, it can cause root rot."

Well, my first attempt at tomato-growing certainly didn't produce a bumper crop. But it did provide some valuable spiritual insights.

Satan is like those worms. Somehow he knows when we're growing and about to bear fruit. He immediately moves in and tries to cut off our blossoms.

We have to be careful how we water our roots. We can get root rot from hearing false doctrines and strange philosophies.

We can compare the first number of the fertilizer formula to hearing the Word of God. If we take in and take in, never doing anything with what we receive and never giving out, we'll go to vine instead of bearing fruit.

The middle number, the one that sets the fruit, is the Holy Spirit. The higher the number, the more fruit we bear. Do you want to be a hundred-fold bearer? Yield to Him 100 percent of your life.

PRAYER: Lord, I want to bear much fruit in my life. Please help me to be careful what I listen to, that I not be misled by unscriptural teaching. Make me aware of satan's devices that would keep my fruit from developing. And help me to be yielded to the leading of the Holy Spirit, that I may bear a bountiful, beautiful crop.

THE PARABLE OF
THE RUDE INTRUDER

Lest satan should get an advantage of us: for we are not ignorant of his devices.   2 Corinthians 2:11

The butterflies in my stomach were flapping around all over the place. I couldn't seem to get them to fly in formation.

Today at noon was to be the first meeting of the Prayer and Share Group the Lord had instructed me to start at work. I had sent notes to several Christians I knew, inviting them to bring their lunch and a favorite scripture they might want to share with others. All morning long I had been concerned. "What if no one shows up?" I worried.

Then I began to be afraid that someone *would* show up. I had never tried to do anything like this before, and I felt terribly inadequate.

As the hands of the clock neared noon, I pleaded, "O Lord, help me. I don't know why You had to get me into something like this. All I can do is my best, but I know that's not going to be good enough without Your help."

I gathered up my sack lunch and my purse. I wanted to get to the room a few minutes early and arrange the chairs in a circle around some tables. I was chuckling to myself about the reaction I had gotten when I had made reservations for the room a few days earlier.

I had told the girl in charge of reservations that I wanted to reserve the room from twelve to one on Friday.

"For what group?" she asked.

"Well, it's for a prayer and share group," I replied.

Silence. Then, "What is the name of the group?" she inquired.

"A prayer and share group," I repeated.

"Oh. That's what I thought you said," she rejoined with a puzzled tone in her voice.

As I started out the door of my office into the reception area, a very irate face loomed in my path. It was a lady from another department who had applied for a position open in my department. She had just found out that someone else had been selected, and she was very unhappy about it, demanding to know why she didn't get the job. I explained that the other person had had specific training and experience in the areas we needed.

"Who do you think you are?" she demanded. "Everybody knows you think you're better than everybody else." She went on and on, with insults heaped on top of accusations.

I kept muttering things like, "I'm sorry you feel that way. I know you're disappointed." Finally, she ran out of steam. Her voice trailed off as she stomped out the door.

Was I glad to see her go! "I certainly made the right decision that time," I was thinking as I inched out the door into the hallway, looking both ways to make sure she wasn't lurking outside, waiting to sock me in the nose.

And then it hit me. There was no doubt in my mind that satan had sent her there at that particular moment to try to upset me and make me even more nervous right before the Prayer and Share Group was to begin. But he had overplayed his hand. In fact, the whole scene had been so absurd that I got tickled. Instead of being discouraged, I was swept by a surge of faith and assurance that God would bring the people He wanted to the meeting, and supply the words I should say. "This is going to be great," I thought as I almost floated down the hall. "If satan is that upset about my starting this group, it *must* be going to be great."

And it was great, as thirteen of us of different races, job levels, and religious backgrounds lunched together and shared our faith.

That day, along with other experiences, has taught me the real value of knowing and recognizing satan's strategies and devices. He seems to be an expert in using other people and circumstances to try to bring discouragement and fear into our lives. But when that happens, we should be *en*couraged, knowing that he sees potential for good in what we are doing. I have learned to consider satan's attacks as a positive sign that I am on the brink of great things for God.

PRAYER: Dear Lord, thank You for the authority You have given me over satan and his strategies. Help me to recognize his ploys instantly, and to thwart consistently his efforts to hinder and bring discouragement.

THE PARABLE OF
THE BUTTERFLY COLLECTION

Where the Spirit of the Lord is, there is liberty.

1 Corinthians 3:17

"Does Wanda still love butterflies?" That was the first question a childhood chum I hadn't seen for years asked my mother.

"I remember she used to have me and all the other kids in the neighborhood out trying to catch them for her," my friend reminisced.

I had always thought butterflies were about the most gorgeous, fascinating creatures I had ever seen. So when it came time to select a nature project for Campfire Girls, collecting butterflies was my first thought. I carefully read the directions in the manual and started out to assemble a spectacular butterfly collection.

I became a familiar sight in our neighborhood with my butterfly net and jar in hand, chasing doggedly after the elusive bits of beauty. A catch would signal a triumphant procession home, net over shoulder and butterfly in the jar held out at arm's length for all to see and admire.

I enlisted my mother's assistance in chloroforming the poor things. I didn't like that part at all, but my doubts about killing them were eased as I saw my growing collection of lovelies, precisely labeled.

Of course, I had to admit they looked strangely and unnaturally still, mounted under glass. I was really aghast, though, the day I took out my collection to show to a friend and found that ants had discovered my prize project. Now they were not only motionless; they were no longer even pretty.

That pitiful sight came back to me recently in contrast to what I was beholding. It was spring, and a volunteer plant was abloom with tiny, fragrant white blossoms near the corner of the house. As I rounded the corner, I was transfixed by what I saw. Flitting from blossom to blossom on that plant were at least a hundred beautiful butterflies,

This time I made no attempt to catch them. I only drank in the exquisite sight. And every time I pass that bush, I see that unique picture in my mind's eye.

Butterflies are not created to be put under glass, and neither are people. We can't constrict others and put them into our mold. And if we could, then they could never become what God created them to be.

PRAYER: Lord, help me not to try to control the lives of others but to realize that people--like butterflies--have to be free. Make me mindful of the fact that even You, the Lord God of the universe, do not try to make us do anything. Rather, You give us freedom to choose--even when our choice is foolish. Remind me that I cannot force anyone else to become more spiritual, and that by trying, I can actually hinder Your work in their lives.

THE PARABLE OF THE WILTED ZINNIAS

Brethren, if a man be overtaken in a fault, ye which are spiritual, restore such an one in the spirit of meekness; considering thyself, lest thou also be tempted. Bear ye one another's burdens, and so fulfil the law of Christ.

Galatians 6:1-2

We had been gone all day, and I hadn't gotten to make my daily visit to see what new, beautiful faces would be added to the collection of flowers I had so carefully tended.

I was especially eager to see the zinnias. The day before, a blossom was just beginning to unfold that looked like it would be an unusually lovely color.

As I rounded the corner of the house, my expectation turned to disappointment. Most of the zinnias had their heads drooped over, their leaves wilted. I almost expected to see them stick out small, panting tongues. They looked terrible!

I was surprised. To be sure, it was the hottest afternoon we had had, after an unusually cool, moist spring. But after all, zinnias are excellent hot-weather flowers. That was the reason I had planted them in that particular bed, exposed to the full afternoon sun.

That very morning, I had read an article about zinnias in the garden section of the newspaper. It talked about what hearty plants they are and how they thrive in hot, dry weather. I thought about getting the article and reading it to those bedraggled-looking posies.

Instead, I decided it would probably be more beneficial if I gave them a little tender, loving care rather than a lecture. After all, they probably hadn't had a chance to get used to such hot weather. I gave them a generous drink of water. An hour later, when I came back to check on them, they were as perky and beautiful as ever.

Too often, we forget that those we look up to in God's Kingdom--strong, mature Christians, who seem to have it all together in their lives--sometimes wilt in the heat of problems and the challenges of living. This is particularly true of ministers and other spiritual leaders, whom we seem to expect to be superhuman creatures, above the frustrations, frailties, and disappointments that the rest of us experience.

It's at those times that we need to give others a refreshing pat on the back and thirst-quenching words of encouragement, not a self-anointed sermon or--even worse--idle chatter behind their backs.

Who knows when understanding and uplifting reassurance might be the catalyst to help another bounce back stronger than ever? And who knows when we might be the ones who need to bounce back?

PRAYER: Lord, give me insight to know when a fellow laborer in Your vineyard needs a special word of encouragement or expression of love and concern. Help me to be one who will hold up another's arms (even as those who upheld Moses' arms) when the burden becomes heavy and human strength falters. Thank You for sending others to help me in times of difficulty and discouragement.

THE PARABLE OF
THE CROSSED-OUT "T"

I can do all things through Christ which strengtheneth me.
Philippians 4:13

"Don't ever even think about saying the word *can't* in this class," I delighted in telling my students. "As far as I'm concerned, that's one of the *worst* four-letter words you could use."

I would write the word *can't* on the chalkboard and then dramatically cross out the *'t.*

"See? There's only one letter's difference between *can* and *can't,* and that difference can make *all* the difference in what you do in school and later in life," I would lecture, getting more and more inspired as I went along. "If you decide you can't do something, you're almost certain to be right; but if you decide to do something, you probably can. I'll help you be successful in the things I ask you to do. I won't ask you to do something unless I'm sure you can do it."

I drummed that message into those kids until they didn't dare tell me "I can't." But I'll have to admit that I cheated a little. I often told a student that I knew he or she could do something, when I really wasn't sure whether that was the case. Of course, I picked things within the realm of possibility, but I wasn't always totally convinced myself. The amazing thing was that, once I persuaded students they could be successful, they always were. There were times when I had to do a lot of encouraging and coaching, but it never failed. If they really believed they could do something, they could. They never let me down.

A real bonus for me was that, after lecturing students so much about *can't,* I could barely use the word myself without feeling guilty.

The result was that I came to realize that God never asks us to do something without equipping us for the task He has given us. Even more important, we don't have to depend on our own talents or strength. How can we fail? When we do our best, we can count on His power to stretch our abilities and make us successful.

PRAYER: Dear Lord, I thank You that You remove the limitations of my human abilities and provide the resources, the ideas--whatever is needed to complete the task You have given me to do. Help me to depend on You more and more, realizing that You are the source of everything good. And remind me to give You the praise and the glory for whatever is accomplished through the work of my hands.

THE PARABLE OF
THE TECHNOLOGICAL AIDS

But they that wait upon the Lord shall renew their strength; they shall mount up with wings as eagles; they shall run, and not be weary; and they shall walk, and not faint.
                                                                            Isaiah 40:31

I felt like crying. After working for more than two hours, writing a speech on the word processor, suddenly, I had lost the whole thing. I tried everything I knew, but I couldn't get the document back on the screen. There was nothing to do but start all over and work faster, since a deadline was breathing down my neck.

"Modern technology!" I muttered to myself. "Who needs it?" I was so mad at that machine, I felt like throwing it out the window. I was just learning to use a word processor instead of a typewriter and was barely comfortable with the process. Evidently I had hit the wrong key, and it had dutifully deleted all of my carefully chosen words.

My reaction to learning to use this high-powered, sophisticated contraption had amazed me. I was completely intimidated by its mysterious intricacies. There was so much to learn--all at once. I would get so bogged down in the procedures of operating the machine that it was difficult to be creative. And talk about frustrating! I would catch myself yelling at the word processor when I couldn't get it to do what I wanted it to. One evening, when I was working late--alone in the building except for the cleaning staff--my not-so-gentle mutterings brought the puzzled face of a custodian peering around the corner into my office. He must have thought I was going berserk.

But finally the complex operations became routine, and the benefits became more and more apparent. The word processor was faster than a mere typewriter. I could use portions of something I had already written in another document without re-keying it, and if I made an error, I could correct it in a minute. Best of all, the ease of editing was conducive to better writing, producing a superior result. The word processor was definitely a better way. I was glad I had persevered and had not gone back to the typewriter.

Sometimes I think that learning to rely on God and to live according to His principles is a lot like learning to use a computer. At first it all seems so different and so complicated.

I am out of sync with worldly approaches. I'm tempted to run out ahead and try to do everything in my own strength and ability. But little by little, I learn that the end result is superior by far when I walk in His way under His guiding hand. Gradually I learn the wisdom of waiting for His strength and leading. And I find that it definitely is a better way.

PRAYER: Dear Lord, thank You for showing me Your better way and for always being willing to exchange Your strength for my weakness, Your wisdom for my foolish thoughts, Your health for my infirmity. Help me to be more consistent as I try to live my life in accordance with Your precepts and principles.

THE PARABLE OF THE NEW CALENDAR

I, even I, am he that blotteth out thy transgressions for mine own sake, and will not remember thy sins.   Isaiah 43:25

Flipping back through the pages of last year's calendar, I saw scrawled notes, lines scratched through, appointments kept, deadlines met. It was messy, sometimes confusing.

I enjoyed removing the pages from the calendar holder and inserting the new pages for the coming year. Into the trash went the old, botched-up calendar. The new, fresh, sparkling-white pages brought a feeling of refreshment and anticipation. It marked a new beginning, a chance to make this a better year than the one before.

And yet I really don't have to wait until the beginning of a new year to have another chance. All I have to do is ask God's forgiveness, and He has a fresh, new, spotless sheet waiting for me. All the old mistakes, the past confusion, the secret transgressions are eradicated, never to appear on my record again.

A new beginning, a second chance? It's available anytime I ask.

PRAYER: Lord, I praise You that Your forgiveness is always available, anytime I ask. Make me mindful of any wrongdoing this day, and eager to confess my failures for Your remission. Thank You for not even remembering my sins of the past. And help me to remember always the importance of keeping my record cleared with You.

THE PARABLE OF THE PUBLISHED ARTICLE

Brethren, I count not myself to have apprehended: but this one thing I do, forgetting those things which are behind, and reaching forth unto those things which are before, I press toward the mark for the prize of the high calling of God in Christ Jesus. Philippians 3:13-14

"Whatever made you think you could write in the first place?" my thoughts chided me as I stared at the cold, heartless rejection slip.

I felt like crying, wadding up the humor piece, and giving up. "What's the use? I've worked so hard, and what do I have to show for it? One published article and a mammoth stack of rejection slips. Maybe I ought to paper a room with them." I was really getting into a genuine pity-party scenario, with me in the starring role.

Writing had always been a desire of my heart. Winning an essay contest and having a poem published in a national anthology in high school had given me encouragement in that direction. Now, for the first time, I was able to devote a little time to writing on a daily basis--at least when I was able to get my three-month-old and twenty-one-month-old down at the same time for their naps.

I looked forward to those creative moments in the afternoon. I enjoyed the mental challenge and appreciated a change from the constant baby talk and diapering.

But as I stared at the manuscript of "And Richard Is His Name," I thought I might as well have been taking a nap myself. *Discouraged* was a gross understatement for what I felt. After all, this was the twelfth rejection slip I had gotten for this same article.

I remembered how much fun I had had writing it. It was a game, trying to make the reader think I was talking about a crotchety old man who had taken over our household. The news that it was really our infant son was carefully kept a secret until the very end. I thought it was very amusing, and the few people I had conned into reading it seemed to enjoy it.

"I might as well toss it in file thirteen," I reflected. "I don't know any place else to send it." But after I got through feeling sorry for myself, I dragged out my *Writer's Market* and started looking for another appropriate magazine to which I could submit it.

I wasn't overly optimistic when I placed the postage on the envelope and mailed it for what I had decided would be the last time. "I'll give it one more shot," I mused, "and then I'll just have to admit it's not funny or clever or any good."

Imagine my surprise and delight when I received from the magazine an acceptance letter--and a check! It was for a small amount, but it represented far more than money. A publisher was actually paying me for something I had written. And the day I received a copy of the magazine containing the published article was one of real celebration.

What if I hadn't sent it out for the thirteenth time? What if I had given up too soon?

How many times does discouragement keep us from a real spiritual breakthrough and blessing that we are on the verge of receiving? Seeing "And Richard Is His Name" in print was a real thrill, but the lesson in perseverance remains a lasting benefit.

PRAYER: Lord, help me not to be discouraged when work I believe You have given my hands to do does not come easily and results appear to be negative and nonproductive. Help me always to look forward to tomorrow, forgetting the disappointments of today. I know that, when I continue diligently and faithfully to perform Your tasks to the best of my ability, You will bless and increase the ultimate results for Your glory.

THE PARABLE OF
THE INTRIGUING SNAKE

There shall not be found among you any one . . . that useth divination, or an observer of times, or an enchanter, or a witch, or a charmer, or a consulter with familiar spirits, or a wizard, or a necromancer. For all that do these things are an abomination unto the Lord; and because of these abominations the Lord thy God doth drive them out from before thee.   Deuteronomy 18:10-12

Jerry was an adventuresome child, always into some kind of mischief. He lived down the street, and his antics were well reported throughout the neighborhood.

We lived outside the city limits. Behind our addition of homes was a thickly wooded area, where Jerry loved to roam, catching frogs, bugs, worms, and whatever else he could find. He always seemed to have a new specimen to display proudly in a jar he carried around with him.

None of the other residents allowed their children to go into the woods because of the large number of snakes that called it home. In fact, it was not unusual to find a snake slithering around in the yard. Usually they were of the harmless variety, but occasionally a water moccasin would find his way onto our property.

Jerry almost caused a neighbor to have a heart attack one day when he emerged from the woods with his latest acquisition. He ran up to her, breathless from his pursuit, and held out the jar, saying, "Look at the beautiful snake I caught!" She was absolutely horrified to discover a colorful red-yellow-and-black-banded reptile--a deadly poisonous coral snake. Fortunately, the jar had a lid on it.

She grabbed it out of his hands and tried to explain to him calmly that he could have been killed by what he considered his prize catch. Of course, he had no idea of the danger he had subjected himself to. He had been intrigued by the idea of having the beautifully colored snake for his very own.

Satan uses the same tactics to try to entrap us and gain an opening into our lives. He lures us with enticements that seem fascinating, fun, and harmless . . . things like reading your horoscope in the newspaper, having your palm read or fortune told at a carnival, or playing with a Ouija board at a party. Many times active church members will ask, "What sign were you born under?"

The Bible clearly warns against such involvement and reveals that it is in satan's realm. We must always be on guard against the wiles of satan. We are warned in 2 Corinthians 2:11 not to allow satan to "get an advantage of us" and not to be "ignorant of his devices."

Just as Jerry should not have been playing in the habitat of poisonous snakes, we need to be very sure that we do not walk on satan's turf by becoming involved in anything that is not of God.

PRAYER: Dear Lord, thank You for the warnings You have given me in Your Word concerning the snares of satan. Help me to realize the importance of learning what Scripture says in this regard and of taking its message to heart. Remind me to be always on guard against allowing any influences in my life that are not pleasing to You.

THE PARABLE OF
THE UNDISCIPLINED FINGERS

Watch and pray, that ye enter not into temptation: the spirit indeed is willing, but the flesh is weak.   Matthew 26:41

As a public school music teacher, I got plenty of practice playing the piano in the course of teaching. I didn't have a piano at home, though, so during the summer months I played very little.

When school started in September, I sat down at the piano and started to play. To my surprise, my fingers were very unruly. I had real problems making them do what I wanted them to. No doubt my brain was sending the correct message to them. They just didn't respond as quickly and as accurately as I expected them to. It seemed as though I had sticks tied to the ends of my hands.

My fingers were undisciplined, out of practice for piano playing. As a result, I had to concentrate hard on making them play the correct notes. And it was impossible to play musically and to interpret the music with feeling, the way the composer intended.

It took several weeks to get my fingers back in shape so that I felt I could really depend on them to respond the way I wanted them to.

It is the same in our Christian walk. Going several weeks without the discipline of prayer and Scripture reading makes it difficult to respond to God's leading and direction in our lives.

PRAYER: Lord, impress upon me anew the importance of disciplining my life. Bring a fresh desire to make prayer, worship, and reading Your Word a vital part of my daily routine. Give me a hunger for the things that would build my spiritual muscles, and enable me to respond instantly to Your beckoning in every area of my life.

THE PARABLE OF
THE BEAUTIFUL ROSEBUD

Let us not therefore judge one another any more: but judge this rather, that no man put a stumblingblock or an occasion to fall in his brother's way.

Romans 14:13

It was so exquisitely beautiful, I simply could not resist it. I purchased the dark, velvety red rosebud and triumphantly brought it home from the grocery store. It was winter, and I missed the fresh flowers that graced our table during the spring and summer months. I enjoyed our evening meal as I glanced often at the elegant, dignified flower.

The next evening as I drove home from work, I thought of the lovely sight that would greet me as I unlocked the kitchen door. Eagerly I opened the door, wondering how much the bud had opened while I was away.

To my dismay, I discovered not a beautiful sight, but a vase turned over, water spilled all over the table, and a rose with drooping petals. I hurriedly placed it in water, but it was too late. It never revived. Evidently my husband had inadvertently knocked over the vase and had left, unaware of what had happened.

That incident preached a mighty sermon to me about our effect on the lives of other people.

My husband did not mean to knock over the vase--but the rose died in spite of the innocence of his intent.

How important it is that we be constantly mindful of our effect on other people. Otherwise, we can thwart the unfolding of a ministry by being critical, judgmental, and discouraging. We can even cause spiritual death or deterioration without meaning to.

It is so important that we be ever aware of our impact on the lives of others and that we be a consistent living testimony of God's love, strength, and care.

PRAYER: Lord, I ask that this day You would help me be an encouragement and an example to each person I meet. Give me a realization of the impact--either positive or negative--that my words and actions can have on the lives of others. I want to be a conduit of Your love and strength. Please show me how.

THE PARABLE OF THE CATACOMBS

According to my earnest expectation and my hope, that in nothing I shall be ashamed, but that with all boldness, as always, so now also Christ shall be magnified in my body, whether it be by life, or by death. For to me to live is Christ, and to die is gain. Philippians 1:20-21

"Why on earth would you want to waste an afternoon in Rome going to look at a place where a bunch of dead people are buried?" our tour conductor asked in a tone bordering on disgust.

"I have a special desire to visit the catacombs. I've always wanted to go there," I explained. "I just can't miss the opportunity now that I'm in Rome."

"It's a long way," she pointed out. "You'd better take the bus. It would cost a fortune to go by cab."

We started out immediately after lunch and found out she was right. It *was* a long way, entailing a transfer to a second bus at the Colosseum. After several problems with communication, we finally found which bus to take and where to catch it. Soon we were passing through the outskirts of Rome, traveling along the Appian Way, the ancient highway built in the fourth century B.C. The dusty brick road grew narrower as we left the teeming city. "Chariots didn't take up much room," I thought as we narrowly squeaked by an oncoming car.

Once at the Catacombs, we were suddenly in the midst of people from all over the world. The crowd was divided into groups by language, and our group was briefed by our English-speaking guide before going underground. We snaked our way through a labyrinth of narrow, twisting tunnels angling off in every direction. The guide emphasized repeatedly the importance of staying with the group. It was easy to see how you could get lost and wander around for hours before ever getting back to the starting point.

The walls of rock were honeycombed with vaults containing the remains of some 60,000 Christians from as early as the second century A.D. Off the main passageways, we entered rooms used for family burials and Christian worship services.

We learned that it had been against the law in Rome to meet freely in groups; but burial societies, by paying a sum of money, could meet to bury their dead. The Christians paid the money and met in the underground chapels for funerals and for the service and feast that followed.

All of this changed, however, when the great persecution of Christians began. Believers were hunted down and put in prison. The Christians started meeting secretly in the underground burial chambers to worship. But soon, even in the dark passages of the catacombs, the Christians' enemies searched for them. The entrances to the catacombs were well known, so the Christians blocked them up and cut new, secret openings. They tunneled through to the sand quarries and opened new exits. When they were surprised at worship, they would flee through the pitch-black, secret passages to the open country.

As we walked in the passageway, our guide suddenly turned off her flashlight. We stood in complete darkness . . . and in complete silence. It seemed that we could almost hear the sound of the fleet sandals of those devout worshipers of long ago echoing down the tiny hallways.

I was amazed at the quantity and quality of art in the small chapels--statues and paintings on the walls, obviously executed by loving hands. We stood before the tombs of Christian martyrs who willingly traded their very lives for the testimony and practice of their faith. Tears brimmed up in my eyes as I heard the stories of these saints of God, knowing that I stood on the exact spot where their feet had trod.

A wasted afternoon? Hardly.

God has brought this experience back to mind time after time. It brings up hard questions. Would I be willing to die rather than to renounce my Lord? Am I less fervent about worship than I might be, since I can worship whenever and however I please? Do I take religious freedom for granted, even as perhaps many of the martyrs of old once did?

I learned from the catacomb Christians that day and I continue to learn from them, even as I do from the examples God has given us in His Word.

PRAYER: Dear Lord, I thank You for the saints of old who walked Your way before us to give direction and to provide an example of commitment and devotion. May I be ever mindful of the tremendous blessing I enjoy in being able to worship You freely and without fear. Help me to love You more, even better than life.

THE PARABLE OF
THE SPEECH IDEA

Commit thy works unto the Lord, and thy thoughts shall be established.   Proverbs 16:3

The thermometer outside read 101 degrees, and my frantic state of mind had almost given me a temperature to match. I had worked myself into an absolute frenzy trying to come up with the perfect opener for the superintendent's speech to principals before the opening of school.

The main theme of his message was the importance of focusing on the overall goals, thrust, and welfare of the entire school district, instead of running their individual schools as independent kingdoms. He wanted to impress on them the importance of keeping their sights on the big picture instead of centering on a narrow, self-serving view.

But how could I dramatize that concept?

I had already fruitlessly searched through every card of my several-hundred-entry speech file and every book of anecdotes on my shelf. A trip to the library also proved futile.

Back in my office, I was engulfed by a sudden wave of self-pity. "What does he think I am, anyway? I'm supposed to come up with brilliant ideas day after day. He gets the accolades, the applause. I just get another assignment, tougher than the one before."

A glance at the clock jolted me out of the dregs of self-pity. Only four more hours. And that included getting the speech typed--if I ever got it written.

I had exhausted every possibility--every possibility, that is, except the most important one.

I put my head down on my desk and said, "Father, You know all the silly gyrations I've gone through today. I've tried, but I simply can't do it on my own. Please show me how I should start this speech."

I immediately thought of reaching for a volume of children's stories on my book shelf, even though I had already looked through the book twice that day.

I gingerly picked up the collection and placed it on my lap. It fell open to Nathaniel Hawthorne's story, "The Great Stone Face." I read with amazement. The story tells about a mountain that looked like the face of a man, but only at a distance. If you got too close, you saw only formless rocks. It was perfect--as if Hawthorne had written it especially to use in this speech emphasizing the importance of maintaining the overall view.

Other parts of the story lent themselves to further analogy and proved tremendously effective in shaping an inspirational challenge. It turned out to be one of the best speeches I had ever written.

Years before, I had committed my work to the Lord. Once again He proved His faithfulness in keeping His promise found in Proverbs 16:3: "Commit thy works unto the Lord, and thy thoughts shall be established." Once more I learned that when I do my part by fulfilling the condition, He is more than ready to fulfill His promise.

PRAYER: Dear Lord, I thank You for Your promises, which I automatically claim and put into action by fulfilling the requirements stated specifically in Your Word. Keep me ever mindful of their power and of the importance of claiming them. I give You praise and glory that time and time again You have been faithful in keeping Your promises.

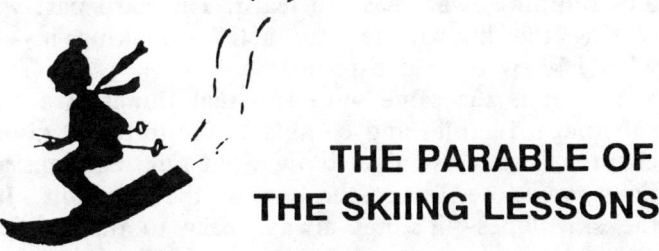

THE PARABLE OF
THE SKIING LESSONS

Be strong and of a good courage, fear not, nor be afraid of them: for the Lord thy God, he it is that doth go with thee; he will not fail thee, nor forsake thee.   Deuteronomy 31:6

"To slow down, you merely point your skis inward, toward each other," the skiing instructor told us as she demonstrated the maneuver.

"That sounds simple enough," I thought, feeling like a creature from another planet, with those heavy, uncomfortable boots and boards on my feet for the first time. "Just make your skis pigeon-toed."

After presenting the theory of skiing and demonstrating the skills, our instructor gave us the opportunity to put it all into practice. Earlier, I had watched experienced skiers fly triumphantly down the big mountain. It looked so exciting, like so much fun!

But now it didn't seem like fun at all. The "baby" beginner slope suddenly seemed bigger than the mountain. I longed to be back at the lodge, looking out the picture window at the breathtakingly beautiful, glistening snow-capped mountains.

It was my turn. There was nothing else to do but go down the slope.

"Just point your skis in," I muttered to myself. Tentatively I pushed off, and almost immediately felt as if I were hurtling down that hill at 100 miles per hour, *plus*. The next thing I knew, my skis were pointing up in the air, and I was flat on my back.

There was nothing about skiing that seemed easy for me. Even getting off the ski lift was a challenge. I did become very good at getting back up on my skis from a prone position. I got in a lot of practice on that maneuver.

The principles of skiing, such as controlling speed and stopping, were easy to learn. The hard part was transferring the knowledge into action--making my body do what I knew it needed to do.

It is the same with spiritual things. We may know spiritual principles and be able to recite them, giving book, chapter, and verse. We know what our reactions as Christians *should* be. But in the heat of the situation--just as on the ski slopes--it's not always easy to put the principles into action.

As I watched excellent, experienced skiers in graceful performance, I noticed that they exhibited correct bodily responses automatically. Obviously they had not learned to do this overnight. It took time, much diligence in practice, and probably lots of spills along the way.

We can also condition ourselves as Christians to respond as Jesus would in the situations we face in life, until our reactions become automatic and consistent. Too, we can learn to remain calm in every trial, knowing that God has everything in hand.

When I started going too fast and getting out of control in skiing, my instinctive reaction was to panic. Invariably, I would tense up, lean backward instead of forward, and end up falling every time.

When we remain in God, leaning on Him, we can remain calm. He gives us His peace . . . regardless of what is happening around us. He provides the calm in the midst of every storm.

PRAYER: Lord, You understand that I know more about spiritual principles than I sometimes evidence in my life. Please help me to implement my head knowledge in day-to-day living, so that it becomes second nature to respond in a way that is pleasing to You. Give me Your peace in every situation, knowing that, when I turn it over to You, it rests in loving, capable hands.

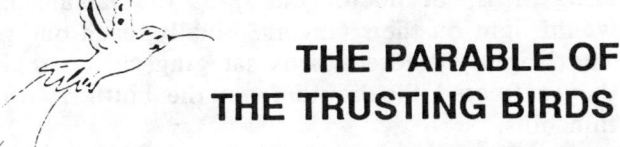

THE PARABLE OF
THE TRUSTING BIRDS

So when they had dined, Jesus saith to Simon Peter, Simon, son of Jonas, lovest thou me more than these? He saith unto Him, Yea, Lord; thou knowest that I love thee. He saith unto Him, Feed my lambs. · He saith to him again the second time, Simon, son of Jonas, lovest thou me? He saith unto him, Yea, Lord; thou knowest that I love thee. He saith unto him, Feed my sheep. He saith unto him the third time, Simon, son of Jonas, lovest thou me? Peter was grieved because He said unto him the third time, Lovest thou me? And He said unto Him, Lord, thou knowest all things; thou knowest that I love thee. Jesus saith unto him, Feed my sheep. John 21:15-17

We sat as motionless as statues, scarcely daring to breathe as we watched a virtual rain of exotically beautiful tropical birds wing their way in to feed. We were sitting on the patio at the Rocklands Feeding Station, located on the west end of the exquisite island of Jamaica.

The birding book belonging to my brother and his wife was absolutely right. Exactly at 4:00 P.M.--as though a dinner bell had sounded--the little lovelies started sweeping in for their dinner. Just outside the covered area of the patio, droves of doves and thrushes joined the smaller diners. In all, there were several hundred birds that came for their daily banquet provided by their hostess of long-standing, Lisa Salmon.

Now in her eighties, this quaint little lady's vision has dimmed, but her eyes still sparkle as she talks about the lovely birds. She tells how she wooed the doves for several years before they finally started coming regularly. But day after day, she continued placing the grain that she knew they liked. Finally they began to come, knowing the food would always be there.

"Put your finger out like this," she demonstrated for my brother and my husband, her finger making a perch. "Then hold the bottle of sugar water at an angle this way. Then don't dare move a muscle." They sat motionless, hoping that one of the exquisite streamer-tail humming birds, or doctor birds, as the Jamaicans call them, would light on their fingers. Finally, each one got his wish. The brightly colored birds sat gingerly on their fingers as they extracted the liquid from the bottles with their long, thin bills.

Then it was my turn. "Put your hands down, palms up, on your legs," Lisa Salmon instructed as she filled my hands with tiny seeds. "The saffron finches feed that way," she explained. Every time some of the gorgeously colored beauties flew into the mountaintop station, I would hold my breath. "Please, come over here," I would hope silently. Finally, several of them nestled in my hands as they pecked for food.

We were amazed that wild birds would actually fly to us and sit on our hands as they ate. Of course, it had nothing to do with us. It was Lisa Salmon who had developed a level of trust over many years in some of God's loveliest creations. They had absolute confidence that she would not harm them and would faithfully feed them every day. No vacations for her in this unusual labor of love.

It was a uniquely lovely experience. I look at the pictures of the tiny birds resting in our hands, and I think of Lisa Salmon's devotion in feeding them day after day, year after year. What motivates her? I don't know. But would that we Christians would desire with equal fervor to feed the Shepherd's sheep . . . and would be as trustworthy in carrying out Jesus' command.

PRAYER: Dear Lord, give me a heart for Your sheep, to minister to others faithfully in every way that You provide opportunity. Make me worthy of the trust of other Christians, and, especially, of Your lambs. Let me not harm them nor lead them astray in any way. I want to be absolutely dependable and trustworthy as Your servant.

THE PARABLE OF
THE SURGING WAVES

Are not five sparrows sold for two farthings, and not one of them is forgotten before God? But even the very hairs of your head are all numbered. Fear not therefore: ye are of more value than many sparrows.   Luke 12: 6-7

We watched in awe as the waves pounded the huge rocks at the base of the seawall. The strong wind wildly punched the water into huge swells topped with billowy bonnets of white foam.

White caps spiraled gracefully upward as if they were ballet dancers leaping into the air in tempo with the sound of the crashing waves.

It was a fascinatingly exciting sight--this power and force of the fury of nature. The dimness of twilight seemed to accentuate the drama being enacted before our eyes. Wonderful to behold from the safety of a car, but disastrous to be at its mercy, I reflected.

I seemed to grow smaller and smaller physically the longer I watched this glorious display. Finally I felt like a mere dot in the scheme of things.

"There's nothing like the ocean or the mountains to help put your own importance in perspective," I said, trying to express to my son what I was experiencing. "We're here for such a brief moment in comparison with their centuries of existence. We're really so insignificant in the total scheme of things, and yet we try to be so important."

I was overwhelmed by the comparison and even more overwhelmed at the realization of how very important, despite our insignificance, each one of us is in the eyes of our Creator. To think that the Lord God of the whole universe unconditionally loves and esteems even me--who am nothing--is much more exciting than watching the waves roll in . . . and more humbling, too.

PRAYER: Dear Lord, I don't understand how You can know and love each of us in such a personal and precious way. But I thank You that You do. Help me to realize that, while I am nothing in myself, I can be a very important person of real worth and value in You. Help me to decrease so that You may increase in my life.

THE PARABLE OF
THE CONFIRMING SCRIPTURE

Which things also we speak, not in the words which man's wisdom teacheth, but which the Holy Ghost teacheth; comparing spiritual things with spiritual. 1 Corinthians 2:13

"Our Scripture for the week is Jeremiah 7:23." Those words brought an unexpected reaction from the guest speaker for our weekly Prayer and Share Group at work. He looked noticeably startled as his head snapped upward.

"Obey my voice, and I will be your God, and ye shall be my people: and walk ye in all the ways that I have commanded you, that it may be well unto you." As I read, I glanced in his direction. There were tears trickling down his cheeks.

We were excited about having Sammy with us. Only a few weeks before, an article in one of the newspapers had told his story. His father had for years owned one of Dallas' most successful and popular supper clubs. It had become a gathering spot for socialites--the wealthy elite. Sammy had grown up in the business and, finally, his dad had signed the club over to him. Neither of them was prepared for the impact that would follow Sammy's acceptance of Jesus as his Savior.

Suddenly the business that had made them rich became the focus of real soul-searching for Sammy and of bitter conflict between him and his father. Most of the profit was based on the "good time" atmosphere they provided, with liquor flowing freely. The drunker they could get their guests, the greater their intake of cash.

Sammy became more and more convicted of the fact that his livelihood was helping satan wreck lives. Finally, he decided to quit serving mixed drinks. His father thought he had gone absolutely berserk. There was no way even a restaurant in that area could compete without booze, much less a place that pulled most of its revenue from a night-club operation.

Bitter words followed. Sammy was adamant; his father, embarrassed and infuriated. His father demanded that Sammy legally sign the club back to him. Sammy refused. After all, his father had given it to him as a demonstration of confidence. Finally, the conflict escalated into a complete breach in the father-son relationship.

As Sammy told his story, the emotional trial was apparent. That very morning he had finally gone to his lawyer and signed the property back to his father. God had told him it was the only way he could restore the relationship. And He had given him a Scripture: Jeremiah 7:23.

Sammy told how he had struggled with that decision, knowing that he was giving up his means of supporting his family, but also knowing that was what God required. "I believe what He has promised me: 'Obey my voice, and I will be your God, and ye shall be my people: and walk ye in all the ways that I have commanded you, that it may be well unto you.'"

As he read, tears again trickled down his cheeks. "When you read that same Scripture earlier," he said to me, "God spoke directly to me and, once more, confirmed the promise He has made to me."

We all were astounded. God ministered to us through Sammy that day, and God ministered to Sammy through us.

While that was perhaps the most dramatic instance, time and time again, I would send out a note containing a Scripture of the Week in advance of our weekly meetings. Then a guest speaker would speak on that same Scripture, or on a thought brought out in that Scripture. Many believed I was calling the speakers and asking them what their subjects would be. But no--it was at the direction of the Holy Spirit that the Scriptures and subjects nearly always matched perfectly.

How wonderful to know that, when we are sensitive to the leading of the Holy Spirit, He will order our thoughts with those of others and bring about a harmony and perfect flow that we could never possibly achieve in our own power.

PRAYER: Dear Lord, I thank You that we do not have to rely on our own limited abilities to decide what is appropriate and best in any circumstance. Help me to have ears to hear what the Holy Spirit is speaking to me and directing me to do. Give me an obedient heart to rush to do His bidding.

THE PARABLE OF THE ELUSIVE BIRDS

Thou wilt shew me the path of life: in thy presence is fullness of joy; at thy right hand there are pleasures for evermore.   Psalms 16:11

"I almost got him that time!" I shouted, placing the salt shaker back in my pocket. Still hopeful, I sat back down on the steps to wait for another chance.

Sparrows chirped overhead. "Come on down here, beautiful birds," I called in my sweetest voice.

I was so sure that this time I would be able to get close enough to throw the salt on their tails. But then I had been sure each time I had tried to sneak up on one of the lovely winged creatures. For an eight-year-old, I was quite persistent. I had been frantically chasing birds all afternoon, and I was hot and tired--but I was determined to get that salt on at least one bird's tail.

"Right over here, little birdie," I chirped.

Just then I heard a snicker from behind the screen door. My brother, six years my elder, was almost doubled up with laughter. He had been watching my unfruitful pursuit and apparently was being royally entertained by my antics.

"What are you laughing at?" I demanded, hands on hips.

"You--you silly goose," he chuckled. "What on earth do you think you're doing?"

"I'm going to catch me a bird," I shouted back.

"Well, you'll never catch one like that," he said derisively.

"I will, too. I almost got the salt on that last one's tail," I pointed out.

"What good would that do?" he questioned. "You'd still have to trap him or something."

"I would not," I said defiantly. "Daddy said that I could catch a bird if I put salt on his tail."

"Silly--he was just kidding you," he grinned.

"No, he was serious, and my daddy always tells me the truth," I argued.

"I know he does, but he was only teasing," my brother said. "Don't you see? If you could get close enough to put salt on the bird's tail, you could catch him without the salt."

Well, I wasn't about to believe any old brother about a matter that serious. I marched inside and asked Mother. To my bitter disappointment, she confirmed what my brother had said.

"But I wanted to catch a bird," I said through my tears. "I would be so happy if I could only catch one."

"What would you do with it?" she asked softly.

"I'd keep it for a pet," I told her. "I'd put it in a cage."

"But then it couldn't fly. And I doubt if it would sing all cooped up," she pointed out. "Why don't you just enjoy watching them and listening to their song?"

"Oh, all right," I agreed, drying my eyes, deciding she was probably right.

I was eight years old when I learned about the futility of chasing birds, but it took several more years for me to learn the futility of chasing happiness. I had to find out the hard way that happiness is not something you can catch and cage or put in a bottle on a shelf.

In fact, I finally have learned that it is not happiness I was seeking after all, but, rather, the joy of the Lord. For happiness depends on circumstances, on what is happening around us, while true joy results from being centered in Him.

PRAYER: Dear Lord, help me to understand the difference between being happy because of worldly things and having Your joy within regardless of the circumstances without. Thank You that Your joy becomes my strength for every situation. Keep me ever mindful of the fact that, when I walk in Your path, Your joy abounds.

THE PARABLE OF THE SCARY CLOWN

Wisdom is the principal thing; therefore get wisdom: and with all thy getting get understanding.　　　　Proverbs 4:7

Big tears rolled down her tiny face as she frantically clung to her mother, burying her head in her mother's skirt.

I felt terrible. After all, I was trying to make her happy, to make her laugh--not scare her out of her wits.

It was graduation night for the clown school I had been attending. For the first time, my classmates and I were decked out in our costumes, zany wigs, and outlandish make-up. We had spent hours and a great deal of effort to come up with just the right outfit to go with the characters we had created.

We were at a large shopping mall. Our assignment? To circulate among the shoppers, talk with the children, and hand out our animal balloons or other trinkets. Afterwards, we would present our skits on the stage in the center of the mall and receive our diplomas.

We soon learned that being a clown was lots of fun and also took a certain amount of wisdom. The song encouraging people to "be a clown, be a clown. All the world loves a clown" proved to be true . . . in most cases.

With young children, however, a clown has to be very careful. Little ones have to be approached cautiously and be given the opportunity to see this strange-looking creature at a distance first. I had to win their confidence. I found out that, instead of going to them, it was better to hold out my little butterfly rings and let them decide to come to me. Otherwise, the experience might end up being a disaster rather than a pleasure.

So too with sharing the gospel of Jesus Christ. We have something wonderful and exciting to offer. But if we come on like gangbusters, we scare people instead of giving them the life-changing and blessed experience that we intend. We have to win their confidence so that they will trust us enough to listen and consider what we have to say.

PRAYER: Dear Lord, thank You for the opportunity to witness to the life-changing power of Jesus. But please, Father, give me wisdom as I try to share the good news. Remind me to depend on Your guidance--not to race out and try to speak in my own power and wisdom. Provide an opportunity this day for me to reach out to another, and I will be careful to follow Your leading.

THE PARABLE OF
THE NEW YORK TRAFFIC

Thus saith the Lord, thy Redeemer, the Holy One of Israel; I am the Lord thy God which teacheth thee to profit, which leadeth thee by the way that thou shouldest go. Isaiah 48:17

We drove into New York City at rush hour on a Friday afternoon. We hadn't planned it that way. Probably no one in his right mind would. But road construction and a huge traffic jam as we approached the metropolitan area had postponed our arrival.

Even so, we really had had no problems--until we saw our hotel. Not knowing on which side of the street we would find it, we were in the wrong lane.

Oh, well. No problem. All we had to do was drive around the block and turn in the drive to the hotel garage. It seemed simple enough at the time, but some twenty minutes later we were still trying to get back to the hotel.

There were one-way streets to contend with. Even streets going the way we wanted to go were obstructed or had a police officer standing defiantly in the middle of the street waving us on. One block stretched into several blocks before we could finally head back in the right direction. Then began the slow inching process of sitting through red lights, green lights, and then red lights again, waiting for the traffic to move. It turned out that our hotel was located near the streets leading to the Holland Tunnel. Everyone in the Big Apple seemed to be headed to New Jersey that afternoon.

Finally, our hotel was back in view. All we had to do was make a left turn, and we would be right in front of it. The problem now was that two huge trucks were blocking the intersection, and traffic was completely tied up. When the light turned green, a couple of cars squeezed into the intersection, making matters even worse. Honking horns and scowling faces added to the mounting tension.

There seemed to be no possible way to turn left-- until a burly truck driver looked our way and indicated that he would let us in front of his trapped vehicle. My son whipped the van around the corner, ending up in a lane for oncoming traffic. Fortunately, the next lane started moving, and the truck driver waited for us to maneuver in front of him. But we were still two lanes away from the curb, and the hotel wasn't far from the corner. Miraculously, the other two lanes cleared just at the right moment, and we were able to turn into the hotel driveway.

How many times have delays in reaching our goals in life caused frustration and irritation? Those goals may seem so close--just out of reach--and yet we can't quite grasp them.

It's then that our patience has a chance to grow, as we continue to be faithful. It's then, also, that we need to seek God to be certain that our goals are in keeping with His plan and purpose for our lives. Once we ascertain that they are, we can be sure He will open the right doors to bring them to fruition, even as the truck driver cleared a path for our van.

PRAYER: Lord, help me to check every area of my life to make certain that my goals are the same as Your goals. Please guide me in staying in the right lane of life and guard me from being swept away from Your purpose by worldly cares and ambition. Thank You that You make a way for me even where there is no way.

THE PARABLE OF
THE MUSHROOMS

Follow peace with all men, and holiness, without which no man shall see the Lord: Looking diligently lest any man fail of the grace of God; lest any root of bitterness springing up trouble you, and thereby any be defiled.

Hebrews 12:14-15

As I walked through the living room, my eye was drawn to an unusual sight in the backyard--two huge, white mushrooms. I could hardly wait to get outside to take a closer look. There they were, looking like elegant sculptures carefully molded by a gifted artist. The green grass accented their whiteness and provided a perfect backdrop for their unusual, fascinating beauty.

They had not been there yesterday. They had sprung up overnight after several days of showers.

Only the day before there had been articles in the newspapers cautioning people against eating wild mushrooms. Several people in the area had been admitted to hospitals after eating mushrooms that had sprouted in their backyard or neighborhood. The articles explained that only an expert can tell the difference between poisonous and edible varieties.

I wondered if these beautiful fungi in our backyard were poisonous or harmless. I was amazed that these intricately formed structures could have grown so rapidly. I learned that they grow from spores which are carried by the wind. Before growth can take place, the spore must fall into a warm, moist place where food is available.

As I examined their form more closely, the thought struck me that a root of bitterness can spring up just as quickly in our lives and can be just as deadly to our spirits as a lethally poisonous mushroom.

Just as I delighted in looking at the mushrooms, we often take a peculiar delight in remembering old offenses and wallowing in self-pity at the thought of slights and in-

77

juries done to us. That kind of mental activity provides ideal conditions for the growth of a root of bitterness. And, unlike the mushroom with its shallow root system, such a plant is not easily toppled.

PRAYER: Dear Lord, help me always to be on guard against unforgiveness, which could cause a root of bitterness in my life. I ask that You bring to my mind even now those whom I need to forgive. Give me the grace to forgive them in order that I, in turn, may experience Your forgiveness.

THE PARABLE OF
THE COMMITTED TALENTS

And God is able to make all grace abound toward you; that ye, always having all sufficiency in all things, may abound to every good work.   2 Corinthians 9:8

"Whatever talents I have, You gave me. I want to use them exactly the way You would have me to. Lord, You made me, and I know You know more about me than I do about myself. Sometimes I don't know what I'm trying to accomplish--always jumping from one thing to another. I offer my abilities to You, God. Do with them what You will, in whatever way is pleasing to You."

It was a simple statement made by the mother of two small children. It was a sincere commitment. I'd never been more serious in my life. I fully expected to get a telegram or something from heaven the next morning telling me where to go and what to do.

But nothing seemed to happen. And yet, through the years, that vow to God has brought astounding results and remarkable opportunities.

I went back to teaching the year our younger child started to school. About two months after school started, I heard that the school district was going to have its own instructional television station. It sounded interesting and exciting. "Too bad I don't know anything about television except how to turn one on," I thought. A few days later, I received a phone call from the superintendent's office, asking me to come to his office.

78

I was surprised and delighted when he offered me the position as coordinator of instructional television for the next year. I enrolled in graduate school that summer and started working on a master's degree in audio-visual education. Talk about having to learn a lot fast! It was a fantastic and, sometimes, overwhelming opportunity. I wrote, produced, and directed programs, appeared as the talent for three elementary literature programs, did lighting and graphics, and served, at times, as cameraman and floor director. I even took the test for a third-class radio operator's license, so that I could act as relief engineer during lunch.

After three years, the Lord directed me to apply for a position with the Dallas schools. I was notified that I had a teaching job even before there was time to check my references. The second year, I applied for the Administrative Intern Program. Shortly after midterm, the phone rang one evening. The assistant superintendent of communications asked if I would like to come to the Administration Building and work for him.

I had never had a journalism course, not even in high school. Suddenly--like a bolt out of the blue--I was transferred and became a professional journalist. I definitely did not have the qualifications or the background. Later, as I was given responsibility for a staff and had to hire others, I was even more amazed. I would not even have considered someone with my lack of experience and training.

Once more, God had sovereignly opened a door. Again, the challenge of learning a completely new field was, at times, almost overwhelming. "Lord, slow down!" I prayed. "After all, this is three completely different professions in three years' time. I'm not sure I can handle it."

His reply? "I have given you these opportunities. I will equip you to handle them." And, of course, He did.

Time and time again, He has put me with people, given me favor, and opened doors for me that I would not even have thought about knocking on. And all because, more than twenty years ago, I committed my abilities to Him and gave them back to Him to be used in any way He wanted.

My experience has proven His faithfulness and His wisdom in providing more and better things for us than we can even imagine or desire. He's far better than any employment agency.

PRAYER: Dear Lord, I thank You for the opportunities that You have given me. Help me always to be faithful to carry out, to the best of my ability, the work You have ordained for my hands to do. I praise You that I do not have to strive or be concerned for the future, knowing that You are ordering my steps and opening the doors You would have me walk through.

THE PARABLE OF THE VANISHING FOOTPRINTS

But we have this treasure in earthen vessels, that the excellency of the power may be of God, and not of us.
2 Corinthians 4:7

It was an astonishingly beautiful day in October--perfect for a day at the beach. The sun shone brightly, but not as savagely as in the heat of summer. The waves frolicked playfully, urged on to greater heights by an autumn wind.

Best of all, the beach was deserted. We had it all to ourselves--except for the permanent, year-round residents. Out on a sandbar, all in a row, sat big-billed pelicans looking as solemn as judges ready to hand down a verdict. Three graceful long-legged egrets stood with heads drooped down, sound asleep in the warm morning sun. Others gazed intently at the water and then darted their long necks downward, emerging with a struggling fish for a mid-morning snack. Seagulls called and flew in to inspect us and our van. Sand crabs scurried among the beautiful seaweed and small, subtly colored shells delivered to shore by the latest wave.

The sensation of the soft sand oozing through our toes was a delight as we waded out into the warm water. The birds didn't seem to mind our presence in the least. It was as though we were one with nature.

Fascinating patterns had been etched in the sand by the coming in and going out of the waves. It looked as though a master sculptor had invested weeks of loving labor to create the intricate, delicately beautiful designs.

The moist sand gave way to our weight as we strolled the beach, leaving our footprints engraved in the fine granules. But not for long. The next wave would erase every trace, leaving no evidence that we had walked that way. It became a game to see how long a footprint would remain. I walked farther from the water, where the waves were not reaching. "These will last for a while," I thought. But, no. The water bubbled up from beneath the surface of the sand. Soon it was all level once more. I walked with heavier steps, leaving a deeper imprint. Regardless of what I tried, my footprints vanished in a matter of moments.

"Just like our worldly accomplishments and attainment of material goods," I mused. "Nothing is lasting unless it is inspired by and ordained of God." I thought of James' comparison of life to a vapor that is here for only a short time and then is no more. And yet we spend so much time and effort building castles of sand as we seek the adulation and applause of man.

My disappearing footprints in the sand remind me that only the things I do for the Kingdom of God will make a lasting impression of my life here below.

PRAYER: Dear Lord, thank You for speaking to me in many ways, even through the things of nature. Give me a greater desire to invest my time and talents in Your work rather than in the temporal, fleeting things of this world. Help me to know and follow Your leading in all that I undertake.

81

THE PARABLE OF
THE YOUNG OPERA FANS

Train up a child in the way he should go: and when he is old, he will not depart from it.   Proverbs 22:6

"We're big enough," Rick declared.

"Yes, Mama," Laurie echoed. "We're big enough."

"You're big enough?" I asked, somewhat puzzled. I wasn't sure what they were talking about, but I was sure they had discussed it and were presenting a determined, united front.

"Yes, to go to the opera with you and Daddy," they shouted, almost in unison.

Every time we went to the opera, they wanted to go too. We had told them over and over that we would take them with us when they "were big enough." I had in mind about twelve years old, but they had decided four and five were better.

"I don't think you'd enjoy it," I explained. "It's real long. You'd have to sit very still and couldn't say a word the whole time."

"That's okay," they agreed. "We'll be so still and quiet you won't even know we're there."

"They sing in another language," I argued. "You won't be able to understand what they're singing."

"We don't mind," they countered.

"There probably won't be any other children there," I pointed out, "certainly not any little children."

"Oh, but we're big," they insisted. "Big enough to go to the opera."

"Well, I don't know . . . "

"Please, Mama, please!" they pleaded.

They met their father at the door with the same argument. We finally agreed to take them, with dire threats about what would happen if they squirmed or talked. I explained the plot to them in the simplest terms possible, sure that they would be sorry they had talked us into letting them go.

Looks of dismay greeted us as we made our way to our seats with Rick and Laurie in tow. I could imagine what fellow opera-goers thought about sitting near two preschoolers. But at intermission, the scowls turned to smiles as we received several compliments on our children's perfect behavior.

The children really did act "old enough" throughout the entire performance, and they insisted that they enjoyed it. They must have, for we were never able to go to the opera again without them.

Now young adults, one is a professional musician and the other an avid fan of classical music. Their exposure to good music at an early age trained their ears to enjoy it.

How much more important it is to train our children to love the things of God. We also can train our own spirits--through the study of God's Word, communing with Him, and having fellowship with other Christians--to desire spiritual things above anything on this earth.

PRAYER: O Lord, make me aware of the importance of training Your children the way You would have them to grow. Help me to realize the impact of my example on my family and on others I come in contact with. Give me the desire to further train the desires of my heart to match the desire and purpose You have for me.

83

THE PARABLE OF
THE TRANSFORMING WORDS

How forcible are right words!   Job 6:25

We were talking about students. That topic inevitably seems to come up whenever two teachers get together. More specifically, we were discussing the impact a teacher can have not only on learning but on the lives of his or her students.

My friend got a faraway look in her eye as she related the story of Robert, a boy she had taught several years before. "He was really a mess," she recalled. "Oh, he had great potential. That was what made it so sad. He just didn't seem to care. Most of the time he wouldn't even hand in a paper or, at best, he would give me a half-hearted effort that wasn't even worth looking at. But every once in a while he would do something really outstanding, and I would see the promise of greatness. I would talk to him occasionally after class and try to inspire him to be all he could be. But I never could seem to get through to him. I don't know why, but he just couldn't seem to get his act together at all. He finally left school, and I lost track of him.

"Then last year during the Christmas holidays, my doorbell rang," she continued. "I almost fainted when I opened the door. There stood Robert, looking wonderful and smiling from ear to ear. I invited him in, of course. What he had to say blessed me but also mystified me.

"'I bet you're surprised to see me,' he chuckled. 'I came home to see my parents for Christmas, and I just had to come by and say thanks.' My puzzled expression was my reply, for he continued. 'You see, I got my degree last spring, and I have a wonderful job. I just wanted you to know that what you said to me turned my life completely around. If it hadn't been for you, I would never be where I am today. I just had to let you know.'"

"What a wonderful Christmas present!" I murmured, sharing a joyful moment with her.

"Yes, it was," she almost whispered. "But the curious thing about it is that I have no idea what I told him. I'd give anything to know what words I said that were potent enough to motivate him and change his life. Believe me, if I knew, I would say the same thing to other students."

My friend's faithfulness in encouraging and pointing the way for her charges had paid off in a dramatic way in the life of one young man. Fortunately, he was gracious and appreciative enough to tell her how much she had meant in his life.

Her experience points out the importance of consistently sowing good seeds in the lives of others by our words, our actions, and our attitudes. We never know when some kindness, or sharing what Christ means to us and has done in our lives, will point the way for someone else and change a life for all eternity.

PRAYER: Dear Lord, thank You for the opportunity to be Your spokesman here on earth. Help me to be a good seed-sower in Your field, trusting You to nourish the words and deeds I sow and to bring them to fruition.

THE PARABLE OF THE SPRAINED HAND

For as we have many members in one body, and all members have not the same office: so we, being many, are one body in Christ, and every one members one of another.
Romans 12:4-5

I should have known better. After all, I hadn't roller-skated in years. But it sounded like fun, and I thought it would all come back to me once I got on the skates. Even before I got around the rink once, though, I hit the floor with a bang. At first, I was more embarrassed than anything else, but then an intense throbbing in my hand signaled that I had hurt more than my pride.

The next morning I went to the doctor and had my hand x-rayed. Only a sprain, he assured me. He wrapped it in an elastic bandage and sent me on my way, with the admonition to keep my hand raised.

Having a bandaged, aching right hand is a frustrating experience for a right-handed person like me. My poor left hand seemed like a tiny child's as I tried to reign it in to write and do other intricate tasks it was unused to performing.

At least I could type fairly well with one hand, but at a very slow, tedious pace. My typing definitely was not keeping pace with my thoughts.

Dressing was another challenge. My husband was called on to zip and button and what-have-you. Cooking seemed nearly impossible.

I had never realized how much I depended on having two hands and how efficiently they worked together as a team. I started telling my right hand how much I appreciated it, hoping that would inspire it to get well and back in operation quicker.

A couple of days after my fall, I had to make a presentation at a banquet. I couldn't find anything to wear that looked just right with a bandaged hand--and having to ask someone to cut my meat for me was humbling, to say the least.

But the sprained hand was a good learning experience. It made me realize how important each part of the body is to the smooth functioning of the rest. A hand is very small in proportion to the whole body; yet without it, the other members are very limited.

And so it is with the body of Christ. With each of us in the place God has chosen for us, fulfilling the role He has ordained for us, a smooth-functioning church can accomplish much for His glory.

I found very quickly that my left hand could not assume the role of my right hand, no matter how hard it tried. As we each find our niche in God's service and faithfully perform the work He has given our hands to do, we find that we make up the harmonious parts that fit together to form a smoothly functioning body.

PRAYER: Dear Lord, thank You for choosing me to fulfill a special place in Your kingdom. Guide me as I seek to be in Your will and to occupy the exact position You would have me fill in Your service. I ask for Your wisdom and vision in the work You have ordained for me to do.

THE PARABLE OF
THE LOVELY VOICE

And the Lord shall guide thee continually, and satisfy thy soul in drought, and make fat thy bones: and thou shalt be like a watered garden, and like a spring of water, whose waters fail not. Isaiah 58:11

I could always tell when the third graders were coming to music class.

Shouts of "Charles, quit pushing," "Aw, Charles," and "Leave me alone, Charles!" announced their arrival. Charles was much larger than the other children. Even though he was in the third grade, he was already starting to grow a little fuzz on his upper lip. He couldn't read and could barely write his own name. Awkward and surly, he could best be described as a "disaster area."

The other children resented him, and little wonder. He was constantly picking on them and doing anything he could think of to irritate them.

But I discovered something about Charles that he didn't even know about himself. He could sing. Charles had one of the most beautiful soprano voices I had ever heard. It was clear and bell-like, and he consistently sang right on pitch.

I started out by letting him sing a solo on one verse of a song in class. He loved it! The other children enjoyed hearing him too. Soon instead of saying, "Aw, Charles," they were saying, "Charles can really sing!" and asking me to let him sing alone so they could listen.

For perhaps the first time in Charles' life, he was getting attention--of the positive kind. His bullying of the other children was growing less frequent.

As Christmas drew closer, I decided to take a big chance on Charles. I asked him to stay for a minute after class. "Would you like to sing the solo in the Christmas program?" I inquired. His eyes lit up as he whispered, "Oh, yes!"

Charles stayed every day after school to work on his part. Since he couldn't read, I had to teach him the words by rote. Just about the time I thought he knew them, he would suddenly forget all he had learned, and we would have to start all over. Finally, just days before the program, he could consistently sing the words correctly.

That evening I held my breath as Charles began to sing. "Oh, Lord, please help him to remember the words," I breathed. A special hush fell over the audience as they listened enthralled by Charles' exquisite rendition of "O Holy Night." To me, it was as though I was hearing an angel sing. It was perfect . . . absolutely perfect.

Charles was never the same after that night. He had a new dignity. He walked with his shoulders back, his head held high. He had found out that he was somebody with something very special to offer.

God wants us to know that we are somebody too--not in our own strength and ability, but in Him--and that we have something very special to offer to lost and hurting people--His love, His power, His grace.

PRAYER: Lord, help me to know who I am in You. I know that You have given me certain abilities and talents. Help me to be faithful in developing and using them for Your glory, knowing that You will increase them and perfect them for Your purpose. Make me ever mindful of the Author and Enabler of all that I will ever accomplish, and careful to give You the glory.

THE PARABLE OF
THE UNPREPARED PLAY

Being confident of this very thing, that he which hath begun a good work in you will perform it until the day of Jesus Christ.   Philippians 1:6

The performance was less than a week away. I was distraught. Of all the plays I had ever directed, this was the furthest from being ready for an audience.

"What on earth am I going to do?" I lamented. I toyed with several possibilities of escape. Maybe I could leave the country. Even a sudden illness seemed like a welcome development at this point.

Postponing the production was out of the question. After all, it was a Christmas play to be given the Sunday evening before Christmas. There had already been articles in the local papers, and many guests had been invited.

"My aunt and grandma and grandpa are coming from out of town just to see our play," one of the children had told me excitedly that evening at church.

"Wonderful!" I had responded, hoping I sounded sincere.

"How did I ever get into this predicament?" I asked myself. The play was a rather ambitious production for a small church. In fact, more than half the congregation was participating. They seemed enthusiastic in the beginning--but that was before the reality of memorizing lines and attending rehearsals really sank in. Few of them had ever been in a play before, so they did not know what kind of dedication an excellent production requires.

There were conflicts with rehearsals. It had proven to be impossible to get everyone together at the same time to practice. And no matter how I begged and pleaded, few had gone to the trouble of memorizing their lines.

"This is going to be a real disaster," I moaned inwardly. "Lord, I have done everything I know to do. I believed it was Your will for me to put on this play, but it certainly doesn't look like it's going to give You much glory. I just hope You can take a disaster and make something good out of it. I'll have to depend on You for the outcome."

As I finished my pitiful prayer, I opened my Bible and immediately my eyes were drawn to Philippians 1:6: "Being confident of this very thing, that he which hath begun a good work in you will perform it until the day of Jesus Christ." I was encouraged, especially by the promise that He would "perform it."

At the next rehearsal, the cast heard my best pep talk, centered around the scripture. "I believe the Lord has told me that He will take the effort that has gone into this play and multiply it, but we have to do our very best."

The dress rehearsal was a shambles. Several still didn't have their costumes, and many still hadn't memorized their lines.

Only that scripture gave me hope that the play would not be a disgrace to the name of God--and that scripture proved to be enough. I was utterly amazed the next evening as the production miraculously unfolded. Not perfect . . . but really good and definitely anointed.

Several people were saved that night as a result of the "good work" that He began and performed.

I learned that, when He begins a good work through me, He will be faithful to perform it when I give Him my best.

PRAYER: Dear Lord, I thank You that I don't have to depend on my own ability. In fact, I would ask You to remind me frequently of the importance of committing all I do to You, knowing that You will take my feeble efforts and anoint and enhance them. Help me to be faithful in putting forth my best, knowing that You will do the rest.

THE PARABLE OF THE EXCELLENT TEACHER

Enter into his gates with thanksgiving, and into his courts with praise: be thankful unto him, and bless his name.

Psalms 100:4

"Wanda, how did you learn how to write?" asked my boss. He had stepped out in faith and given me a job as a writer, although I did not have the credentials for the position.

"I really don't know," I reflected. I puzzled over the question, which I had never considered before. "Oh, yes I do!" I declared with sudden revelation. "It was Miss Eula Pearl Smith, my junior year in high school. She taught me the tools of writing and how to use them with precision: how to make transitions from one paragraph to another, how to organize my thoughts and get them down in an interesting and orderly fashion. She was quite a teacher-- hard as they come, and absolutely determined that her students were going to learn to use the English language correctly and precisely."

Later, as I mused over our conversation, I was glad my boss had asked that question. It gave me pause to contemplate just how much I owed to Miss Smith, a teacher of rare dedication and ability. Not only had she taught me; she helped me to discover a talent and encouraged its development.

After we had studied poetry, our assignment was to write a sonnet. When our sonnets were completed, Miss Smith kept me after class one day and told me I should enter my sonnet in a poetry contest for high-school students.

"It's really well written, very expressive," she assured me. My self-confidence soared when it was published in a regional anthology of high-school poetry and then was chosen for the national anthology.

Next, she encouraged me to enter an essay contest for Dallas students. I won a $25 bond that time. Later, as I ventured timidly out as a freelancer and started accumulating a mountain of rejection slips, I was encouraged by those recognitions in high school. "I won those awards in high school, didn't I? Someone thought I was a good writer." I held on tenaciously to that thought as I tried again.

Not long after that, Miss Smith came to a meeting at the School Administration Building. I met her in the hallway and had the opportunity to tell her, face-to-face, how much she had meant in my life and career and how very much I appreciated what she had done for me.

If I had given her a million-dollar check, it would not have made her happier. She fairly beamed. I felt wonderful, too, knowing that I had given much-deserved praise and recognition and had expressed my thankfulness to one who had given enormously of herself to me as well as to thousands of other students.

I thought of others I had not thanked and cannot thank because they are no longer here on earth. And I realize that I also am often negligent in thanking my heavenly Father for His countless blessings, faithfulness, and unfathomable love.

Miss Smith and I were both pleased that day because I said thank you, just as God is pleased and we are blessed when we praise and thank Him for who He is and for what He has done in our lives.

PRAYER: Dear Lord, I take so much for granted. Help me to develop a spirit of thankfulness, so that I will be faithful to acknowledge the countless blessings You bestow on me. I give You praise and glory for all You have done, for all You are doing this day, and for all You will do in my life in the future.

THE PARABLE OF
THE UNSEEN COMPUTER CODES

Howbeit when he, the Spirit of truth, is come, he will guide you into all truth: for he shall not speak of himself; but whatsoever he shall hear, that shall he speak: and he will shew you things to come. John 16:13

I just couldn't figure it out. I was trying to print out a document from my computer, but it just wasn't working right. It was single-spaced, with double spaces between paragraphs--but right in the middle of the page was a gigantic hole of about twelve to fifteen lines. The printer dutifully printed the last few lines of my letter at the top of a second page.

Having had strange and mysterious problems with computers in the past, I panicked. My new one had been working perfectly and--aside from having to learn a whole new system, resulting in somewhat of an information overload for my poor brain--there had been no significant problems.

"I'll try it again," I thought rather apprehensively. "Maybe the paper didn't feed through the printer exactly right." My second attempt produced identically disappointing results.

Finally I decided there must be a stray code embedded in the text somewhere. I hit the video key that revealed on the screen all the codes the computer is obeying in printing a document. Without the video, those functions are not displayed, but they are nevertheless there, making their impact on the result.

Sure enough, about halfway down the page, I found the culprit. Apparently I had unconsciously hit a key I hadn't intended to. All I had to do was delete the code, and all was well. The letter printed out perfectly.

Often we don't understand circumstances around us because there are spiritual forces at work that we cannot see with our natural eyes. The Holy Spirit is the video we have available in spiritual matters. He will guide us and give us insight into the workings of the spiritual world surrounding our natural world. He also will help us to understand how our present situation relates to what is to come in our lives and individual ministries.

PRAYER: Dear Lord, thank You that I do not have to lean on my own limited understanding when it comes to spiritual matters. Fine-tune my ears to hear that still, small voice of the Holy Spirit as He brings enlightenment and direction for my walk with You. And, once I understand that direction, give me the desire and the ability to be obedient to His leading.

THE PARABLE OF
THE MOSAIC PICTURE

And he shall sit as a refiner and purifier of silver: and he shall purify the sons of Levi, and purge them as gold and silver, that they may offer unto the Lord an offering in righteousness. Malachi 3:3

We watched in fascination as the mosaic-studio artist in Florence, Italy, tediously filed away at the tiny pieces of marble with his miniature tools. We were in awe of his patience and skill in making the small bits interlock smoothly. Time and time again, he would try the pieces and then continue the smoothing process until they fit perfectly into the marble mosaic picture his hands were creating.

Finally, after much concentrated effort, he was satisfied with the result. He then turned the picture face down and applied two different types of hot resin or glue to set the pieces firmly in place. The back of the picture was ugly . . . a huge mess.

Ah, but when he turned it over, everyone gasped with delight. They saw an exquisitely beautiful picture made from dozens of small pieces of naturally colored marble.

Nearly everyone who watched the picture take final form had to have one of the lovely mosaics to take home. That evening, as I looked at the one we purchased, the Lord showed me that our lives are like that mosaic picture.

God is the artist. Only He knows what the picture is to look like. Only He has the overall plan to fit all the bits and pieces together in the right way.

The filing hurts, and we don't really enjoy His removing things from our lives that hinder our spiritual development. We definitely don't like the hot glue He applies to cause us to stick to His plan.

Often we don't understand what's happening and why He's permitting a certain experience or problem in our lives. That's because we're looking at the back side, or we're up too close to see the total picture.

But the exciting thing is that, if we will let Him and will stay out of the way, He will create an exquisite masterpiece with our lives. My souvenir from the mosaic studio is an encouraging and continuing reminder that God's purpose in my life is constantly being fulfilled.

PRAYER: Lord, help me to recognize that it is Your hand that is shaping me and refining my life and character to conform me to the image of Your Son. Give me patience as You bring people and situations into my life with purpose. Give me a firm realization that the end result will be a masterpiece, if only I will give You liberty to complete what must be done.

THE PARABLE OF
THE OVERCAST DAY

For we walk by faith, not by sight. . . . But without faith it is impossible to please him: for he that cometh to God must believe that he is, and that he is a rewarder of them that diligently seek him. 2 Corinthians 5:7; Hebrews 11:6

What a disappointment! Here we were, finally, in Acadia National Park, and visibility was very limited. The rain came down intermittently, but the haze and fog were with us constantly. Several people, when they learned we were going to Maine, told us to be sure to see Acadia, which includes the more than forty square miles of Mount Desert Island, the largest rock-based island on the Atlantic Coast.

The island is a unique coming together of the exquisite beauties of nature. The Atlantic Ocean has carved coves and inlets among the fingers of land reaching out into the water. The huge, craggy rocks of various hues and colors provide a stark contrast to the foam of the breaking waves. There, so close to the ocean and granite cliffs, are the ancient rounded peaks of the Mount Desert Mountains.

Standing as a benign overseer of this magnificent scene is the 1,530-foot Cadillac Mountain, the highest point on the Atlantic coast of the United States.

At least we knew the mountain was *supposed* to be there. We just had to take the travel guide's word for it. Because of the fog, we couldn't even see the huge mountain. We stopped at the Visitor's Center to learn more about this gem of nature, and got a map showing the various points of interest. We passed the road sign that pointed the way up Cadillac Mountain. No use to take that road. We knew that the fog would be worse as we went higher. So we journeyed on to other points by the ocean, hoping that the sun would suddenly pop its radiant face through the blanket of clouds.

Every place we stopped was exquisitely beautiful--with the mist creating almost a surrealist painting. We took pictures, hoping that our cameras could capture the moody landscapes we were seeing.

The next morning, to our delight, the fog had lifted and the sun was shining in all its glory. We lost no time in getting to the summit of Cadillac Mountain. What a magnificent view! You could see for miles and miles-- quite a contrast to the day before. We drove along some of the same roads we had traveled then. We saw the same scenes, but in a different light--brighter, more intense. They were beautiful both days . . . but in different ways.

Our lives are like that too. Some days, everything seems to go right, and God seems to be abundantly blessing everything we do. Other times it seems that we are surrounded by darkness and, despite our best efforts, nothing turns out right.

There are times when God seems to be far away and not concerned about what we are going through. At those times, we have to walk by faith, taking the word of the Guidebook, even when we don't see God's hand at work in our lives.

The pictures we took those two days in Acadia remind me that there is beauty in dark days as well as in brighter moments, and that the Creator of that beauty is always present, just as that mountain was, even when it was hidden from our view.

PRAYER: Dear Lord, I thank You that You are ever present. Help me to increase the measure of faith You have given me, so that I can walk by faith moment by moment even when I see no evidence of results in my life. And in hours of darkness, Father, help me to know and to experience the beauty of Your love.

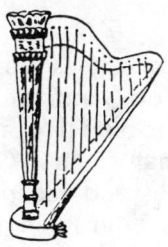

THE PARABLE OF
THE HARP STRINGS

Whatsoever thy hand findeth to do, do it with thy might; for there is no work, nor device, nor knowledge, nor wisdom, in the grave, whither thou goest.   Ecclesiastes 9:10

The package contained a new set of strings for my daughter's harp. She had been eagerly waiting for them. The old ones had become brittle, and she never knew when the next one might pop . . . perhaps right in the middle of a performance. They had cost about $280--a small investment for the peace of mind they would provide.

But they still would do her no good until she could find the time to attach each one carefully at the top and the bottom to the pegs in the harp. A loose string would not produce music. She also had to be sure to put each one where it belonged. The strings for the higher notes would not fit in the lower range. They would be too short. The strings for the lower notes were not only too long for the upper range; they were also made of metal, which would produce a different effect entirely.

After the strings were all in place, the delicate process of tuning had to be done. Each one had to be stretched to just the right tautness in order to produce the desired note. And they had to be tuned several times before they would finally hold their pitch. New strings have to be seasoned for a few days before they finally settle down to staying in tune.

As Christians, we are like those harp strings. We may have much to offer for the Kingdom of God. But we too must be disciplined. We must find our place, the part

He would have us play. We also must be willing to be trained and stretched and shaped, even though sometimes the process is tedious and uncomfortable. Last of all, we must prove our faithfulness by being good stewards in the specific tasks we are given to do.

Only then can we make beautiful music in God's symphony.

PRAYER: Lord, help me to be patient as You stretch and secure me in the place where You want me. Take away any desire I might have to run to and fro and to seek a position of my choosing rather than Yours. Give me faith to know that my daily experiences and the people I come in contact with are all a part of Your plan to season me for the work You have chosen for me to do.

THE PARABLE OF
THE SPUNKY SPARROWS

I have fought a good fight, I have finished my course, I have kept the faith: henceforth there is laid up for me a crown of righteousness, which the Lord, the righteous judge, shall give me at that day: and not to me only, but unto all them also that love his appearing.   2 Timothy 4:7-8

The neighborhood birds had discovered my backyard feeding station. Usually there were several birds perched among the seeds, busily dining to their hearts' content. They were interesting little creatures and proved a fascinating entertainment while we ate our own meals and watched from the kitchen window.

There were several kinds of birds that came to dine. I was always thrilled when the beautiful pair of cardinals added their crimson color to the setting. The bluejays also presented a spectacular sight in their blue-and-grey feathery suits. All of the birds were beautiful--each one in its own way.

Even the grackles, the bullies of our dinner guests, displayed gorgeous, iridescent green feathers on their heads as a kind of crown to their black-draped bodies. They were usually the largest birds and came zooming down in groups of five or six. Even before they landed, the other birds would scatter. In an instant, the grackles would be left to dine undisturbed.

However, there was an exception--a couple of spunky sparrows. Oh, they scattered with the rest of their kind, but they would take up an observation post on a nearby fence. There · they waited patiently until the grackles settled down to their feeding. The feisty little fellows would then wing their way downward and gently settle among the much larger grackles. They weren't going to be intimidated out of their meal by those noisemakers. Interestingly enough, the grackles never bothered them in the least.

Those two sparrows had made-up minds. They had decided to eat, and eat they did. They learned to stand against the obstacles--in this case against half a dozen birds that were at least ten times larger than they were.

As Christians, we need to get spunky like those sparrows. We need to set goals of commitment and never permit ourselves to be swayed from our purpose, regardless of the size or nature of the obstacles.

PRAYER: Lord, help me to have a made-up mind to serve You and to seek the things that honor and glorify You in my life, regardless of the obstacles. I know You are not pleased with a double-minded person. Help me to live a holy life, dedicated to Your purpose.

THE PARABLE OF "NO PROBLEM"

And we know that all things work together for good to them that love God, to them who are the called according to his purpose. Romans 8:28

"No problem." We first heard the phrase on our way to Ocho Rios from the airport. Our bus driver rounded a curve on the narrow, twisting road and almost collided head-on with a car speeding down the middle of the highway. There were audible sighs of relief from the passengers as he swerved just in time. "No problem," our driver said in a jolly tone of voice.

"Wow! Does he have a relaxed outlook!" I thought, reflecting on the reaction such a risky maneuver would have elicited from most American motorists.

We soon learned that "No problem" was the unofficial national slogan of Jamaica and an almost universal attitude among the people. During our week-long visit, we must have heard the phrase hundreds of times. No matter what happened, the sweet-natured, easygoing people of Jamaica saw "no problem."

The phrase seemed to be uttered not only with their lips but from their hearts. Whether it was disappointment that we didn't want to buy any more carved birds from the street vendors or the dashed hopes of a ragged little boy who wanted a tip for walking along beside us on the street, the response was always the same--"No problem," said sincerely, with a broad smile.

I was charmed by their outlook, and reflected on a trip we had taken to Europe a couple of years before. I had made up my mind before we left that absolutely nothing was going to mar my enjoyment of a journey I had looked forward to for years.

And nothing did. Not even rude people who obviously resented Americans, but were glad to take our money. A bus breakdown that delayed us. A controversy between the smokers and non-smokers on the bus. A man who berated me for at least five minutes for setting my purse on the back of his car. A motorcyclist who ran into me and was ready to hit me for getting in her way. Almost getting knocked down in the jam-packed airport in New York City by an impatient woman who kept jabbing me in the back with her bag. There was "no problem" as far as I was concerned during the trip through seven European countries. I had adopted that attitude and I stuck with it throughout the month.

Back home from Jamaica, we found that "No problem" had become a part of our conversational pattern, too. Every time I hear the phrase or say it, I think of the Jamaican people and how much I want to be like them in their calm handling of the disappointments of life.

And why shouldn't I be unruffled and unflappable in every situation? After all, God has everything under control. I have committed my life to Him, and I have His promise that, regardless of what may happen, He will shape every situation, each circumstance, for my ultimate good. He will exchange beauty for ashes, His strength for my weakness, and praise for a spirit of heaviness. In Him there truly is "No problem." He's bigger than all problems.

PRAYER: Dear Lord, I thank You that You are the answer to every problem I face in my life. Help me to rest in the assurance that You are working all things together for good--even when nothing seems right or makes sense. Enable me to turn every care, every concern over to You so that I truly can have the serenity of a "no problem" attitude.

THE PARABLE OF THE METICULOUS PALEONTOLOGISTS

To them who by patient continuance in well doing seek for glory and honour and immortality, eternal life. Romans 2:7

Tedious! That was the best word I could think of to describe the work of the paleontologists suspended on scaffolds and hunched over the sandstone cliff, their work area day after day, week after week. Their tools were tiny chisels and other small implements as fine as any surgeon's instruments.

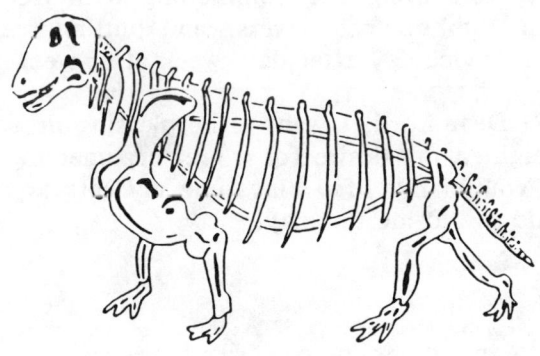

We were visiting Dinosaur National Monument, which covers 325 square miles in Colorado and Utah. It contains one of the world's largest concentrations of fossilized dinosaur bones. Many silicified bones of brontosaurs and other species of prehistoric creatures have been removed from a single sandstone cliff here. Several entire skeletons have been quarried and reconstructed.

An unusual feature of the monument is the visitor center built around the cliff containing the dinosaur bones. Visitors can be seated in cushioned chairs in air-conditioned comfort to watch the work of the technicians as they patiently and minutely chisel away with loving care. Because of the age and rarity of the bones, the paleontologists must take great pains in chipping out the sandstone encasing them. Their goal is to expose the bones in high relief rather than remove them. Through the years, technicians have exposed more than 1,200 fossilized bones on the quarry face.

I watched in fascination, not only because of the skill of the workers but also because I realized we were in the presence of unusual people, totally dedicated to and engrossed in their painstaking task. I wondered just how long it would take to reveal the complete shape and dimension of the bones being worked on that day. While I certainly didn't envy them their work, I definitely admired their commitment and determination. Obviously it didn't matter to them how long it took. They were bent on digging out those bones.

That's the kind of devotion and resolve we must have if we are to live the Christian life successfully. We must be consistently digging in the Word for truth and direction, worshiping and communing with God, having fellowship with other believers, and putting feet on our faith with service day after day, week after week.

PRAYER: Dear Lord, I want to be pleasing in Your sight. Please heighten my desire for a greater, unerring commitment to You in my life. Fine-tune my ears to hear what You would say to me this day.

THE PARABLE OF
THE CHANGED STUDENT

For the Lord God will help me; therefore shall I not be confounded: therefore have I set my face like a flint, and I know that I shall not be ashamed.   Isaiah 50:7

I was simply overwhelmed. My first year of teaching was not at all what I had envisioned. I had conjured up this very unrealistic picture of eager students waiting with anticipation to learn all I had to impart to them. I was shocked to discover that most of them did not seem interested in learning and that I had to work very hard just to whet their appetites.

I was teaching in a small school, with grades one through twelve all housed in one building. My assignment was demanding, to say the least. In the mornings, I taught a high-school speech class and two first- and second-grade music classes, then worked with the high-school chorus. After lunch, there were six more elementary music classes. In all, I taught more than five-hundred students, besides directing the junior play, the senior play, and the one-act play for competition. I also put on several musical programs during the year.

Not knowing much about children of any age, I found it particularly difficult to adapt my approach, in a matter of minutes, from teaching teenagers to teaching first graders. Being a city girl in a small town for the first time was also quite an adjustment.

One evening I told the students in the play I was directing that I would take them home after rehearsal. In the high school I had attended, all the students lived within a small radius of the school. It did not occur to me that one student would live eight miles in one direction, another ten miles in the opposite direction. By the time I had deposited the last student safely at home, I had driven more than seventy miles. As I headed for home, my car got stuck on the muddy dirt road in pitch blackness. By the next morning, everyone in town had heard that the new teacher had had to leave her car out in the country and hitchhike back to town.

I was determined to be a success as a teacher--but in spite of my frantic activity and best efforts, I sometimes felt I was a dismal failure. The only positive thing was that I was praying more than I had prayed in a long time.

Toward the end of the year, things were getting easier, and I was no longer being mistaken for a high-school student. Students were progressing in spite of my inexpertness and inexperience. I was beginning to decide that maybe I could be an effective teacher after all.

The real payoff came in a sixteen-year-old student named Mary Nell. On the first day of school, I had asked the students in my speech class to stand up, introduce themselves, and tell what the highlight of their summer had been. When Mary Nell's turn came, she almost fell on the floor. I was scared out of my wits, thinking she was having a heart attack or something equally disastrous.

After class I found out that she was so frightened, her legs were like rubber. Mary Nell had had polio as a young child. The only lasting impairment was a slight limp, which I hadn't even noticed. But to her, it was a huge disability that made her feel ugly and awkward. She had one of the worst inferiority complexes I had ever encountered. I worked with her on her self-concept and tried to give her extra encouragement.

Little by little she grew in confidence. Toward the end of the year, the speech class gave a play for a school assembly. Mary Nell turned in a beautifully poised, commanding performance in the leading role. As I watched her that morning and realized how she had blossomed since the day I first met her, I knew she had been worth it all-- every discouraging moment and all the hard work.

I had set my face as flint to be a good teacher, and the Lord had helped me and blessed my faltering efforts. Suddenly I really felt as though I had earned the right to be called a teacher.

That year, I probably learned a great deal more than I taught. One of the greatest lessons was not to be dismayed when faced with an overwhelming task, but to rely on God, with His unfailing strength and help, to increase the effectiveness of my sincere effort.

PRAYER: Dear Lord, thank You for always being ready to help me when I call on You. I praise You that You can take my struggling effort and add the yeast that makes it rise to accomplishment and worth in the lives of others. Help me to remember always to give You the glory for whatever You accomplish through this earthen vessel.

THE PARABLE OF
THE FIG TREE

Ye shall know them by their fruits. Do men gather grapes of thorns, or figs of thistles? Even so every good tree bringeth forth good fruit; but a corrupt tree bringeth forth evil fruit. A good tree cannot bring forth evil fruit, neither can a corrupt tree bring forth good fruit. Every tree that bringeth not forth good fruit is hewn down, and cast into the fire. Wherefore by their fruits ye shall know them.

Matthew 7:16-20

"That tree is doomed to die," our jungle-tour guide proclaimed dramatically, his soft Spanish accent taking a little of the edge off the pronouncement.

We gazed at the bizarre-looking tree whose trunk extended upward at least twenty-five to thirty feet. The curious thing about it was that other trees, contorted in shape, hung from its branches. Some of them were already rooted firmly in the ground; others had roots reaching earthward.

105

The guide explained that the danglers were a type of fig tree that grows in that area around Puerto Vallarta, Mexico. It starts out on another tree as a parasite, without any roots of its own. Before long, it starts growing roots, which finally extend to the ground and attach themselves in the soil. Finally, the host tree becomes surrounded by roots, and it is choked by the trees that began in its own branches. The interloper figs eventually cut off the necessary moisture and nourishment from the roots of the host tree, and it dies.

The gnarled, grotesque fig trees produce fruit, but it is not fit for human consumption. The birds, though, eat the figs and drop the seeds. These attach themselves to other trees as they are dropped, and the destructive process begins anew.

I looked with sadness at the tree, imagining how stately and beautiful it must have been before the bad seeds were deposited in its branches.

And I couldn't help but wonder. What kind of seeds am I sowing in the lives of others? Seeds of destruction that maim and destroy, or seeds of encouragement and hope that help others to grow into the beauty that God intended?

PRAYER: Dear Lord, I want to be a bearer of good fruit in my life. Help me to be consistent in sowing good seeds both in my life and in the lives of others. Give me keen sight to spot any weeds that may sprout up to choke healthy growth. Assist me as I try to be faithful, so that I may produce a bumper crop of excellent fruit.

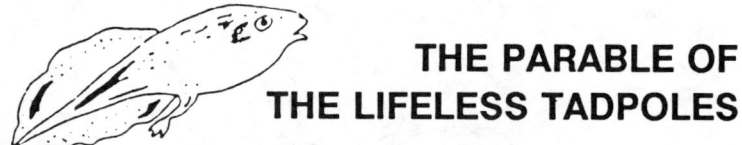

THE PARABLE OF THE LIFELESS TADPOLES

My people are destroyed for lack of knowledge: because thou hast rejected knowledge, I will also reject thee, that thou shalt be no priest to me: seeing thou hast forgotten the law of thy God, I will also forget thy children. Hosea 4:6

"Mama, there are some real little black things swimming around out in the ditch," two-and-a-half-year-old Ricky announced, breathless with excitement as he burst through the kitchen door. "I don't know what they are. Come, see."

He grabbed my hand and pulled me out the door. He then trotted ahead as fast as his short legs would go to his favorite crawfish fishing spot in the drainage ditch in front of our house. His eyes danced with anticipation as I got down on my knees to take a closer look.

"What are they, Mama?" he asked insistently.

"Why, they're tadpoles," I answered with surprise.

"Tadpoles? What's that?" he wanted to know.

"Well, they're baby frogs. At least, they'll turn into frogs when they're grown," I explained.

"Really?"

"Hey, Ricky! How would you like to watch them turn into frogs?" I asked, already knowing the answer.

"Wow!" he exclaimed.

We raced into the house and returned to the ditch with a strainer and a jar. I filled the jar with water as he swished the strainer, trying to catch the swift-moving tadpoles. No fisherman could have been prouder of catching a six-foot swordfish than Ricky was when, after several tries, he trapped a tadpole in the strainer. A few minutes later, we were back in the house and Ricky was triumphantly watching his two tadpoles eat the bread crumbs he sprinkled on the water.

I got down the encyclopedia to find out what to expect. I decided the tiny amphibians must be about one month old and learned that, in about another month, they would start to grow small hind legs. Then, over the following three to four weeks, those legs would lengthen, their front legs would grow, and their faces would change to look like a frog. After that, they would absorb their tails, and the metamorphosis would be accomplished.

Every morning, first thing, Ricky would run to see if the tadpoles had changed during the night. He almost popped open with excitement when he saw the first foot start to emerge. It was an interesting experience for the whole family. Even his little sister was toddling in every morning to see the "fwogs."

Finally, the pair had all four legs, and they looked like frogs. Absorbing their tails was all that remained for the transformation to be complete.

But one morning, I heard a shriek of despair from the kitchen. Ricky had found the little frogs floating on top of the water--dead. What a disappointment! Unfortunately, the encyclopedia didn't explain that, at that point in their development, they could no longer breathe indefinitely under water. And so they had drowned.

Ricky was inconsolable. I felt terrible. "If only I had known," I reflected, "I could have placed some rocks around the edges for them to jump on top of."

Just as the frogs perished because of my lack of scientific knowledge, our souls can perish for lack of spiritual knowledge. Our experience with the tadpoles points out the importance of learning and understanding God's principles, not only in the natural realm but also in the spiritual realm. With such understanding, we can live life abundantly according to His plan.

PRAYER: Dear Lord, please increase my desire to study Your Word so that I may accurately apply Your spiritual principles in my life. Help me study to show myself approved in Your sight, and assist me in speeding up my spiritual development.

THE PARABLE OF
THE SOBBING STUDENT

But as we were allowed of God to be put in trust with the gospel, even so we speak; not as pleasing men, but God, which trieth our hearts.   1 Thessalonians 2:4

Horace's body shook uncontrollably, he was sobbing so hard. He looked very small as he sat there in the school office, waiting to see the principal.

Horace was a special-education student. He was awkward in movement and a slow learner. But an even greater handicap in relating to the other students was a rather severe speech impediment. He had great difficulty in being understood.

Unfortunately, it was the type of handicap that brings out a cruel streak in some children. They teased Horace unmercifully whenever a teacher wasn't around, often mimicking his strange sounds and halting attempts at communication.

It was just such an incident that had brought him to the office, awaiting whatever fate the principal would mete out. Horace finally had gotten fed up with one of his most persistent taunters. He lashed out with fists and feet, leaving his tormentor with bruised shins and a bloody nose.

I sat down in the chair next to Horace and placed my hand on his shoulder. "What's the matter, Horace?" I asked as kindly as possible. He looked up to see who was talking to him. He tried to say something, but he was crying so hard that it was even more difficult than usual for him to speak.

I handed him a Kleenex. "I'd like to help if I could," I offered. He looked so miserable, my heart went out to him.

"John . . . John . . . was making fun of me," he sobbed in barely decipherable syllables. "He kept on and on. And I hit him . . . hard." He paused with the most forlorn look I had ever seen. "Nobody likes me," he moaned.

"But, Horace, that's not true," I assured him. "I like you."

He looked at me pitifully for a moment and then let out an even louder sob. "But you're just a teacher!"

I couldn't refute that, and I understood. What was important to him at that moment was not what "just a teacher" thought, but how his peers felt about him. That's only natural as a child develops his self-concept and tries to find his niche. But as he grows up and matures, he learns to set standards of his own and to value the opinions of those he looks up to and respects.

The same is true of maturing Christians. We should be looking increasingly toward God and seeking His approval rather than trying to find favor with man. Realizing that the standards of God, as delineated in His Word, are often diametrically opposed to the standards of the world, we should not be surprised when resistance, criticism, and even ridicule come our way.

PRAYER: Dear Lord, my desire is to be pleasing in Your sight in all my ways. Help me to look to You rather than to man for direction and approval. Give me the boldness to speak and live the truth of Your principles, even when I know they will not be popular in the sight of man.

THE PARABLE OF
THE SPRINTER AND THE PLODDER

Wherefore seeing we also are compassed about with so great a cloud of witnesses, let us lay aside every weight, and the sin which doth so easily beset us, and let us run with patience the race that is set before us. Hebrews 12:1

"It's a difficult decision to make," my colleague lamented. "I have no choice but to cut one position. But which one?"

She went on to explain that she had narrowed it down to two employees--two good employees who were entirely different in their approaches.

"I really like them both," she sighed. "They're both good people. I just hate to have to do this to either one of them."

"What are their strengths . . . and their weaknesses?" I questioned, trying to get her to focus on facts rather than the turmoil she was experiencing.

"Well, I guess if I had to describe each of them with just one word, I would name one 'the sprinter' and the other one 'the plodder,'" she mused. "The sprinter is more enthusiastic and has really creative ideas and approaches. She can inspire people and get them excited, too. The problem is that a lot of times she starts a project with a bang, but doesn't bother to take care of all the necessary details. All of a sudden I'll find out there are a lot of loose ends dangling. Then I'll either have to assign someone else to help complete the job or step in myself. I have to check on the sprinter often to be sure everything's going along okay."

"What about the plodder?" I asked.

"The plodder really isn't as talented or dynamic," she observed thoughtfully. "But he's consistent. When I give him an assignment, I know it will be well-planned down to the last detail. He follows through, even if it means working way past quitting time. I never have to check on his progress or wonder if a project is going to fall apart."

"Which is more important to getting the work of your department done? Talent or dependability?"

"Well, they're both important," she answered thoughtfully. "But realistically speaking, with fewer employees, I'm going to have less time to supervise each one. It will be less time-consuming to help the plodder come up with creative ideas at the onset than to have to be constantly checking up on the sprinter and pulling the chestnuts out of the fire. Looks like I'll need to go with the plodder."

It was an interesting conversation. Later, I asked a friend who owns an employment agency what he thought of her decision.

"I would go with the plodder, too," he said. "Sprinters just don't hold up too well in the long haul."

Maybe that explains why it appears sometimes that God chooses unlikely people to do His work. He doesn't always select the most talented or the most dynamic--at least, not in my opinion. But, of course, He knows a lot of things about them that I don't.

He knows all about their faithfulness and about their obedience in doing His bidding. He's tried them before in smaller assignments with lesser responsibilities. He knows what they will do in difficult situations and in times of discouragement.

He too seems to choose the plodders, rather than the sprinters.

PRAYER: Thank You, dear Lord, for past occasions to do Your work. I want to be found faithful in all things, knowing that if I want to be given mighty deeds to do in Your kingdom, I must prove my consistency and reliability in small things first. Help me to be Your good and faithful servant in each task You grant me the opportunity to do for You.

THE PARABLE OF
THE GREEN LIGHTS

Every valley shall be exalted, and every mountain and hill shall be made low: and the crooked shall be made straight, and the rough places plain.   Isaiah 40:4

I was running late. It had been one of those mornings when nothing had worked right. The clock radio had not come on, and from that point on, everything had gone downhill.

Usually it would not matter much, but today I had an 8:00 A.M. meeting. The superintendent, a stickler for starting right on time, would be presiding, and I really didn't relish the idea of slithering in late.

I ran out to my car. Wouldn't you know it? The windows were all fogged up. Another delay as I rushed around the car wiping them off.

As I started the car, I murmured a plea to my Father. "Lord, I know it's not Your fault I'm running late, but I need Your help if I'm going to get to my meeting on time. You know how many traffic lights there are on my way. It sure would help if they would be 'go lights' instead of 'stop lights' today."

By this time I was approaching the first of about twenty traffic lights on the route I took to my office. It was red but, just as I started to put on the brakes, it turned green, and I sailed right through.

The same thing happened time and time again. I would think, "I'm going to be caught by this one for sure." But then, just at the last moment, the light would change to green. What usually was a twenty-five- to thirty-minute trip was trimmed to about eighteen minutes. I was absolutely amazed and, by the time I arrived at the school administration building, I was overwhelmed with praise.

I rushed into the building and found a seat at least one minute before the meeting began.

All green lights on my way to work had never occurred before, nor has it since. I don't know what the mathematical probability of such an occurrence would be, but the odds are bound to be very high.

Getting to the meeting on time was wonderful. Even more wonderful is knowing that my heavenly Father loves me so much that He would overcome such odds to save me embarrassment. It's exciting to have the assurance that He is always ready to help in a crisis situation. But in a way, it's even more exciting to know that He cares even about the small details that are important to me.

PRAYER: Dear Lord, I thank You that You are the God of the impossible and unlikely. I give You praise and thanksgiving for the numerous times You have demonstrated Your power for me in the situations of this life. I rejoice that You are with me in every facet of my life--in moments of grave importance and even down to the tiniest details.

THE PARABLE OF
THE PAINFUL BACK

The liberal soul shall be made fat: and he that watereth shall be watered also himself. Proverbs 11:25

I was creeping slowly through the living room, surveying the distasteful scene. The house and I were both a mess-- the aftermath of three days in bed with flu.

I was just thinking about how much I had to do and how little energy I had to do it when, all of a sudden, a sharp pain pierced my lower back, locking me into a bent-over position. I tried gingerly to straighten up, but it was no use. I could not release myself from my stooped posture, try as I might. "What next?" I thought with a sudden surge of self-pity.

Regardless of how I felt, I had to go see my aunt. Recently she had had to go into a nursing home, and I was the only one who could see to her needs.

I went--but grudgingly, I must admit. I kept thinking about all I had to do. And my back hurt every step of the way.

When I got to the nursing home, my aunt needed some items from the drugstore. Reluctantly, I ran the errands for her, getting in and out of the car at each stop with greater difficulty.

113

Returning from doing her shopping, I found her in a mood that just about matched mine. She was lonely there without her friends. The food was terrible. The people weren't friendly. Her roommate was hard to get along with. In fact, nothing pleased her. She was having one big pity party.

I started talking with her about how good God had been to her, how He had kept her through the years in good health and with plenty of this world's goods. She nodded in agreement as I continued.

"You have something that is priceless that some of these people don't have. You have Jesus. You can reach out to them in love in His name. And when you allow yourself to be used as a channel for God to meet the needs of others, He will automatically meet your needs--without your even asking."

Suddenly there was a light in her eyes as she murmured, "That's right. That's right."

But something happened in me also. The moment I made the statement, the pain in my back left. I needed to hear my own words and know that the promises in Isaiah 58 are true. There, the prophet speaks of first meeting the needs of other people and then says, "Then shall thy light break forth as the morning, and thine health shall spring forth speedily: and thy righteousness shall go before thee; the glory of the Lord shall be thy rereward" (v.8).

I hobbled into the nursing home that day. But I floated out.

PRAYER: Lord, I ask You this day to make me aware of the needs all around me and to give me a burning desire to help others. Make me forgetful of my problems so that I may concentrate on reaching out in love to comfort, encourage, provide in whatever way is needed. Give me insight into the situations others are facing, and Your wisdom to know how to help them.

THE PARABLE OF
THE PUZZLING CHICKENS

Without counsel purposes are disappointed: but in the multitude of counsellors they are established.   Proverbs 15:22

"What do I do now?" I asked my husband, looking with frustration at the chicken I was trying to cut up and cook for Sunday dinner.

We had been married for three weeks, and I didn't exactly feel at home in the kitchen. I had cut off the fryer's legs and the wings, but was at a complete loss to know what to do next. My husband came over, peered at the solid-appearing body, and shrugged his shoulders. "I have no idea," he laughed.

"Well, I don't either," I muttered as I started hacking away. It seemed like forever before I finally got the chicken cut into parts small enough to fry. At least I knew, more or less, how to fry a chicken. My husband was hungry enough to eat the chicken whole by the time I finally got it on the table.

"Uh, what part of the chicken is this?" he asked with mischief in his eyes as he pointed to one of the strange-looking pieces. I wasn't exactly in a jocular mood, but I had to admit it was pretty funny. We had a good laugh over our first fried-chicken dinner.

His aunts raised chickens, and they had given us enough to fill the small freezer in our refrigerator. The next Sunday, I told my husband it was his turn to cut up the chicken. I giggled as he seriously approached the challenge. If anything, his results were even weirder than mine had been. We had chicken each Sunday for several weeks. We took turns wielding the knife, with consistently comical results.

A few months before we got married, my mother had volunteered to show me how to cut up a chicken. At the time, I really wasn't interested. "Thanks, anyway, but I'll just buy mine already cut up," I had retorted. Needless to say, the next time I went home, I very humbly asked my mother to show me how to cut up a chicken. She did it with such ease--the result of many years of experience.

How often in our Christian lives are we faced with a similar situation? We know what the end result is that we want in a particular area of our lives. We have seen others who exhibit that characteristic--perhaps joy or peace. It looks so easy for them. But we don't know how to go about making it a reality for ourselves.

It's then that we need to go for counsel to those who can point the way and show us how to achieve the desired result.

PRAYER: Dear Lord, I thank You for the counselors You have provided for me in the past to demonstrate and teach me how to walk in Your way. Bless them, Lord, for the time, love, and prayers they have invested in my life. Help me to be humble enough to seek the counsel of those with greater spiritual maturity.

THE PARABLE OF THE BAFFLING CANYON

One thing have I desired of the Lord, that will I seek after; that I may dwell in the house of the Lord all the days of my life, to behold the beauty of the Lord, and to enquire in his temple.   Psalms 27:4

Our first trip to the interior of Mexico was proving to be a delight. We were enchanted by the beauty of the land and the nature of the people. While staying in Monterrey for a week, exploring the city and making side trips to nearby spots of interest, we had spent one day in the exquisite town of Saltillo. Another day, we had driven to the top of an especially scenic mountain and had gone through a cave high on the mountain's side.

The third day we set aside to visit Huasteca Canyon, for our travel book gave a vivid description of its unusual beauty. We decided to take some food with us and have a picnic in this exquisite creation of nature.

The map indicated that the canyon was about two miles off the main highway near a small village. It was not far from Monterrey, so we anticipated being in the canyon within half an hour. As we drew close to the tiny village, all four of us started looking closely for a sign indicating the road to Huasteca Canyon. We looked and looked, but saw no sign.

Soon we were several miles past the village, still looking for a sign. Finally, we decided to drive back into the village and see if we could get directions.

"¿Señor, por favor," I stumbled in my rusty Spanish to the first likely looking pedestrian, *"donde está Huasteca Cañon?"*

He smiled broadly, nodded his head, and started spewing out a string of words that left my mind spinning in incomprehension. However, he did point toward a small dirt road to his left, so I assumed that was the way to go.

"Gracias," I murmured uncertainly, climbing back into the car.

"I'm not sure, but I think he said to go down that road," I told my husband.

"That road?" he asked. "Why, that's little more than a cow trail!"

"I know, but I think that's what he said."

We started out, bumping along, thankful that it hadn't rained lately. Finally, the road just petered out. No canyon there. We turned around and snaked our way back to the highway.

Two or three trips back up and down the highway produced not a single clue as to where the canyon might be. I tried to ask someone else, but he only shrugged his shoulders.

We were getting a little discouraged in our quest, when someone made a suggestion. Why not measure the distance on the map from Monterrey, apply the scale, and see if we could find a road at that exact point? We drove back to the city and started looking for a road exactly 8.2 miles down the highway.

Sure enough, there was one. We turned left and started down a dirt road. Soon we saw a woman walking along with two children. I rolled down the window, pointed ahead, and asked, "Huasteca Canyon?"

"Si," she replied with a warm smile.

We drove for what seemed like a long way on the narrow, twisting road. At least it was better than the first road we had ventured down.

Suddenly, there it was--an exquisitely beautiful jewel nestled among mountains encircling it. We drove around the perimeter of the canyon floor, enchanted by the ever-changing panorama of shapes and colors. The startling silence was broken only by an occasional song of a bird as it flew overhead.

We were as one with creation and our Creator as we walked amid the rocks and vegetation. Our lunch tasted unusually delicious. The day turned out to be a real highlight of our trip--well worth the effort it took to seek out and finally find the elusive canyon.

The things we seek spiritually sometimes seem even more difficult to arrive at than Huasteca Canyon. We would have missed a wonderful experience if we had not set our minds as flint to find the canyon. How much more tragic to miss spiritual blessings because we have not made up our minds never to give up until we attain what we desire from God!

PRAYER: Dear Lord, help me to be stubborn in my resolve to grow spiritually and to do Your will. Teach me to throw off discouragement and not to be sidetracked by the attractions of this world. Please give me a hunger and a burning desire for You and Your kingdom.

THE PARABLE OF
THE STARVING EGRETS

Oh how great is thy goodness, which thou hast laid up for them that fear thee; which thou hast wrought for them that trust in thee before the sons of men!   Psalms 31:19

"It was so sad! To see them staggering toward the fountain, their eyes glued to the ground searching for the tiniest movement of an insect. And then they would just keel over and die. Hundreds of them."

My brother's wife was talking about the beautiful white cattle-egrets they had seen on their visit to the Dry Tortugas, a remote island about sixty-five miles off Key

West in the Gulf of Mexico. Martha and Larry are avid birders and had joined several other birding enthusiasts on an unusual journey to this bird-lover's paradise.

They talked animatedly about their trip by seaplane, about camping on the beach, and about the fascinating species of birds they had seen. But with a sad expression on their faces, they always came back to the plight of the starving egrets.

I shared their sorrow, having always been fascinated by the long-legged birds with their graceful, curved necks. They are a common sight wherever there are cattle. I had seen them many times, not only following the cows around, but also riding on their backs.

The winged creatures are instinctively attracted to the Dry Tortugas as a resting place on their way to the mainland. The uninhabited island has water and seems a natural place for them to stop, eat, and refresh themselves. It's a virtual haven for many varieties of other birds, but it invariably becomes a grave for the cattle egrets.

Why do the egrets starve to death, while all the other birds thrive? Because of the egret's ingrained habit of always looking on the ground for its food. That's the reason the egret hangs around cattle. He waits for the cows to stir up insects in the grass and leaves.

There are no insects on the ground in the Dry Tortugas--but there are plenty of them in the trees. The unfortunate egrets are so accustomed to looking down-- never up--that they don't see the food readily available to them with a few flaps of their wings. And so they grow weaker and weaker and finally die.

People are like that, too--when they put their confidence in man and worldly position and possessions rather than in God.

Oh, things may seem to be going along all right for a season, but sooner or later we all find ourselves in situations where material things cannot provide the answer and others let us down. It's then that we're especially thankful we have learned the wisdom of looking up to God rather than limiting our vision to the things of this world.

PRAYER: Dear Lord, more and more I want to look to You rather than to temporal things. Help me to realize that the things of this world are fleeting, while the things of Your kingdom are everlasting, never-ending. Give me heavenly vision to see and concentrate on the things above--not on those below.

THE PARABLE OF THE WRONG TARGET

Woe unto you, scribes and Pharisees, hypocrites! for ye are like unto whited sepulchres, which indeed appear beautiful outward, but are within full of dead men's bones, and of all uncleanness. Even so ye also outwardly appear righteous unto men, but within ye are full of hypocrisy and iniquity.

Matthew 23:27-28

A small crowd was starting to gather. Much to my surprise, I was the center of attention. On a sudden impulse, I had decided to stop at the archery range on my way home from work. I hadn't picked up a bow and arrow since college, and I wanted to see if I could still hit the target.

Archery was one of the few things I had discovered in the realm of sports that I was pretty good at, and I had enjoyed it when I took it in physical education.

120

I tentatively picked up the bow, inserted the arrow and pulled back on the string. Zing! To my surprise, I hit a bull's-eye on the very first try. I tried another with the same amazing result . . . and another and another.

By this time other archers were abandoning their own targets to watch my astounding performance. My efforts were greeted by applause and comments such as, "She's really good!"

"Why don't you join our archery club?" one invited.

Even though I must admit I was enjoying the attention, I was absolutely mystified by what was happening. You see, I was aiming at one target . . . but consistently hitting the center of the target next to it. But I wasn't about to tell any of my admirers of the slight flaw in my performance. I triumphantly paid my fee and left.

I couldn't wait to get home and find a picture of an archer in the encyclopedia. The mystery was solved when I discovered I had been placing the arrow on the wrong side of the bow.

How many times do we fool others by our outward performance as Christians? We may appear to do and say all the right things, secretly knowing that our motives and heart attitudes are not really what they seem to be on the surface. We may fool others, but not ourselves . . . and certainly not the Lord.

PRAYER: Dear Lord, help me to make my heart attitudes and motives match what I say. I don't want to just put up a *front* of righteousness; I want to *be* righteous. But You know, Lord, how easy it is for me to slip into putting on an outward show. Guard me against falling into that kind of trap, and please caution me when I am headed in that direction.

THE PARABLE OF
THE WRONG-WAY DRESS

The Lord God hath given me the tongue of the learned, that I should know how to speak a word in season to him that is weary: he wakeneth morning by morning, he wakeneth mine ear to hear as the learned.   Isaiah 50:4

"What a gorgeous dress!" I almost said aloud as I paused in browsing through the dozens of frocks on sale. It was pure silk and a beautiful print of burgundy, blue, and shades of brown--colors that could be worn year-round.

The price was unbelievably low and, unfortunately, so was the size. A size 4 was marked on the ticket. Since I wear a size 8, I looked at the label in the dress just to be sure there was no mistake. No, "Size 4," the label also proclaimed. It *looked* large enough though, and it hung in soft pleats from the yoke to be belted in at the waist. It was certainly worth the few minutes it would take to try it on.

I slipped into the dressing room, eager to see if I could fit into the elegant garment. Yes, it fit perfectly-- except it seemed uncomfortably tight around the sleeves, and I wondered about a tie at the back of the neck. I took it off to try on some other dresses I had selected. But after I had finished, I went back to the silk dress. "I really would enjoy wearing that dress," I thought. I tried it on once more, but finally decided it was just not comfortable.

A woman who had seen me looking at the dress earlier asked me if I was going to buy it. If not, she said, was interested in it for her daughter. "No," I replied, handing it to her reluctantly. "It's just too tight around the sleeves. I guess I was optimistic to think I could squeeze into a size 4."

She looked carefully at the dress. "Which is the front?" she wondered aloud. "I believe the tie goes in the front."

"Really?" I asked. "I tried it on with the tie in the back. Maybe that's the reason it didn't fit right."

"Would you like to try it again?" she graciously asked, offering the dress.

"I really would--if you don't mind," I replied enthusiastically.

She seemed almost as pleased as I was when I showed her how perfectly the dress fit--after I put it on the right way. Later, I wondered why I hadn't been able to recognize the front of the dress.

I never wear that dress without thinking of the kind lady who showed me the right way to wear it. I also think of the importance of being equally kind to people who are seeking the right way in their lives, but are having a problem in knowing which way to go. Our taking

122

a moment to point the right direction, to share a scripture, or to demonstrate the love of God may be all a person needs to get him or her started on the right track.

PRAYER: Dear Lord, I thank You for those You have brought into my life to point the right direction spiritually when I didn't know which path to take. Help me to recognize those You now bring into my life who need direction, and give me Your wisdom in providing godly counsel.

THE PARABLE OF
THE MINOR KEY

Wherefore, beloved, seeing that ye look for such things, be diligent that ye may be found of him in peace, without spot, and blameless. 2 Peter 3:14

It was Christmas Eve--always a time filled with anticipation and bustle. Each year we looked forward to the midnight service at our church. But this year would be special. Our ten-year-old daughter was going to play her harp in church for the first time.

Our whole family was very much involved. I was the music director and organist. My husband sang in the choir. Rick and Laurie would sing in the Children's Choir at the family service at 8:00 P.M. Laurie would play the harp for that service and also for the more elaborate, traditional midnight service, which would usher in Christmas Day.

She went over her piece several times during the day. "I want to play beautifully," she said with intense feeling.

Knowing she was a little nervous, I held my breath as the blessed strains of "Silent Night" were plucked from the strings of the harp during the eight o'clock service. She did play beautifully and received a number of very nice compliments. She was so buoyed up by her success and the kind words of encouragement that she could hardly wait for the second service to begin.

There was about an hour between services--too little time to drive home and back again. We waited and relaxed in the pastor's office. Laurie kept bouncing in, wanting to know if it was time yet.

Finally, the second service began with the regal procession of the Adult Choir. Laurie confidently waited for her cue and began playing with aplomb. But the sound was, to say the least, unexpected. Obviously she was playing "Silent Night"--no one could mistake it--but in a minor key.

I peered over the organ to see a very puzzled expression on her small face. My husband and I looked at each other with concern, trying to figure out what had happened. Laurie plodded through the piece with a look of consternation.

It was only after the final note of the recessional had sounded that the mystery was solved. Between the services, someone--probably a child--had entered the church and fooled with the pedals of the harp. A couple of the pedals had been pushed down, making those two notes flat. Fortunately, the piece still sounded all right, although very strange, in a minor key.

It hadn't occurred to Laurie, nor to us, to check the pedals before she played. Needless to say, that's one thing that quickly became a part of her routine before a performance.

Part of *our* routine as Christians needs to be a daily check for sins of commission or omission that can cause discord in our lives. Lack of attention to prayer and reading the Scripture, allowing wrong attitudes to creep in, dwelling on unholy thoughts, reading or watching ungodly material--all of these can throw us out of harmony with the Lord and with His purpose, causing us to live life in a minor key.

PRAYER: Dear Lord, please help me to be attentive to the small things that can bring about disharmony in my spiritual life. Give me a hunger for You, so that my days will be filled with melody beautiful to Your ears. Bring to mind my sins of omission and commission, so that I may immediately receive Your forgiveness.

THE PARABLE OF
THE VULTURE

Submit yourselves therefore to God. Resist the devil, and he will flee from you.   James 4:7

They circled ominously above the valley, their huge wings outstretched as they glided in the cool mountain breeze. Occasionally they interrupted their smooth flight with a few slow flaps of their powerful wings.

"Beautiful, they're not," I thought as I looked through binoculars at their crimson, naked and warty heads, aesthetically much too small for their bodies. Their hooked beaks added to their odd appearance. Once on the ground, they displayed humped backs as they walked slowly and clumsily toward their prey.

I was surprised to learn that, in spite of its menacing appearance, the vulture is very weak. That's the reason it will not attack a living creature. With its unusually sharp eyes, it carefully selects a dead animal, or seeks out one that is near death. Then it hovers about, waiting for its last breath.

Vultures have especially frail legs and claws. The encyclopedia says that they have "weak bills fitted only for tearing decaying flesh" and "blunt claws which are poor weapons for seizing and carrying off their food." Obviously the scavenger recognizes his limitations and operates within those parameters.

Sometimes satan seems to be strong and powerful. But he also knows his limitations. He will not attack in the areas of our lives where we are alive in the Lord. He looks for a spiritually dead part of us and strikes there. He knows that he is too weak to overcome us in places that are under the lordship of Jesus Christ.

In 1 John 4:4, we read: "Ye are of God, little children, and have overcome them: because greater is he that is in you, than he that is in the world."

RAYER: Lord, I thank You for equipping me to live an overcoming, victorious life in You. Help me to keep my life so centered in You that I do not become a prey for satan's attack in any area. But when attack does come, help me to remember to use the power that You have given me, as a believer, over the evil one.

THE PARABLE OF
THE FLABBY MUSCLES

And let us not be weary in well doing; for in due season we shall reap, if we faint not. Galatians 6:9

I casually tossed my towel over the weights on the exercise machine, trying to look as nonchalant as possible. I didn't want all those physical-fitness buffs to see that I had to set the machine on the lowest possible weight.

I had really been embarrassed, on my first visit to the physical-fitness center, when the instructor took me through the program to show me how each of the weight-resistant machines worked. Even on the lowest setting possible, I had to use both arms to move one of the weights.

To say I was out of shape was to make a gross understatement. Never the athletic type, I spent my days sitting at a desk. Evenings and weekends were gobbled up by running a household, shopping, and juggling an array of responsibilities at church.

Exercise? Even if I had the inclination, where would I find the time? But then the Lord started dealing with me about my physical fitness . . . or lack of it. My commitment to shape up had brought me to the center three days a week after work.

It all seemed so awkward . . . and so difficult. Those muscles really rebelled. They had had it too easy for too long to rejoice at what they were being forced to do.

Just four weeks later, to my amazement, I had gone from being able to do only ten sit-ups to twenty-eight, had increased the weights on the leg machines by twenty pounds and on the upper-body machines by ten pounds. I could even do both arms at one time on the machine I had found most difficult.

Best of all, my energy level increased dramatically, and I was more alert mentally. The exercise and physical challenge also helped to release tension.

I really surprised myself one day when I picked up a large iron skillet with my left hand--something I had not been able to do since I had sprained it severely in college.

I walk up to one of the leg machines and see that the man who used it before me had it set on 150 pounds. I think: "I'll never be able to do that. That's an unattainable goal." I set it back to 50 pounds . . . to what seemed like an unattainable goal only a few weeks before.

That's the way it is with spiritual growth. God shows me an area of my life that needs correcting, and I work hard to overcome the problem. Once I seem to get on top of that one and breathe a sigh of relief, He has a new challenge waiting for me--some flaw I have never seen in myself before.

Sometimes I think I'll never be able to lift the spiritual 150-pounder. But then I look back to where He's brought me from, and I can rejoice and praise God for where He's taking me to.

PRAYER: Lord, I thank You that the things that are impossible to do in my own strength are possible through Your power. I appreciate Your showing me the areas in my life that need to be changed and, most of all, Your helping me to make those changes. I pray for Your continued strength and encouragement as I press toward the mark of being all You created me to be.

THE PARABLE OF
THE MISSING SCULPTURE

For whatsoever things were written aforetime were written for our learning, that we through patience and comfort of the scriptures might have hope. Romans 15:4

It was a classic case of impulse buying. We were in a showroom in Florence, Italy, in an establishment with a long-standing reputation of excellence in fine crystal and glassware. We had watched with fascination as the glass-blower produced an exquisitely beautiful vase before our eyes.

We had no intention of purchasing anything. We were there only to look and enjoy the visit along with other members of our party. But then we saw it--an enchanting crystal sculpture that instantly and simultaneously intrigued my husband and me. It was quite modern in form. As we moved and looked at it from different angles, it seemed to change into quite another shape before our eyes. And the brilliance! It sparkled in the light from the windows and changed color as it was moved into different shadings of illumination.

We agreed that it was the perfect remembrance of our trip and would add a lovely touch of elegance to our home. We also found that it had a perfectly outrageous price--but suddenly that didn't seem to matter. Surprising ourselves, we wrote a check. Of course, it would have to be shipped to us. The owner told us that it would probably be at least two months, maybe somewhat longer, before it arrived.

We excitedly told friends and relatives about the gorgeous sculpture. But as the weeks stretched into two months and then three, we began to wonder. All we had was a receipt and a canceled check. What if they didn't send it? What could we do?

My mind raced back to a time in Mexico when we had ordered a wrought-iron bench and paid for it to be shipped to us. It never arrived, and the letters I wrote went unanswered.

We also began to wonder if the sculpture was really as beautiful as we had thought. We couldn't even remember exactly what it looked like.

Finally, we received notice that a package had gotten through customs and had arrived in Dallas. My husband said he would pick it up. He was going to bring it by my office so I could see it before he took it home. I could hardly wait.

My excitement ended instantly with a phone call. My husband had opened the package. But instead of finding a sparkling crystal sculpture, he saw only a pile of soiled children's clothes. "They said they would try to locate it," my husband said disappointedly. Since the package was addressed to us, we weren't too optimistic. We were convinced that, somewhere during the complicated process of shipment from Italy to the United States, someone had seen the sculpture and had thought it as beautiful as we had. In my imagination, I pictured the thieves exchanging the pile of dirty clothes for our beautiful masterpiece. I could even imagine it gracing someone else's living room.

But still we hoped against hope that our package would be found. In the meantime, we talked about having spent too much on it in the first place and vowed that we would never again have something of value sent to us from another country. Several days later, though, our hope became reality when a phone call brought the good news of the package's arrival. My husband went to the station again, and this time returned triumphantly with our treasure.

It really is as lovely as we had remembered it, and we continue to be uplifted by its beauty. Fortunately, our hope was justified and fulfilled.

The exciting news, though, is that, when our hope is fixed on eternal values and firmly rooted in the Word of God, we do not have to be anxious about the outcome-- not even for one moment.

THE PARABLE OF
THE MESSY MAKE-UP

Search the scriptures; for in them ye think ye have eternal life; and they are they which testify of me.   John 5:39

What a mess! The orchid greasepaint was smudged over into the white, and the black ran over into all the wrong areas, making dingy gray patches.

I hadn't put on my clown make-up for a while, and it was not going well. "That's strange," I muttered. "I've never had this much trouble with it before."

I reached for a tissue and tried to wipe off the top layer, but it only made matters worse. It seemed that whatever I did only resulted in a bigger mess. I was about at the point of taking all the make-up off and starting completely over when I glanced at the clock. No time for that.

I was about to panic when, finally, I realized what I was doing wrong. I had forgotten to dust on an ample amount of baby powder after I had applied each color. "Of course! That's it!" I almost shouted to myself, thrilled to have finally solved the mystery. The powder set the greasepaint and kept it from running when another color was applied.

It also kept the make-up from rubbing off on my clown suit, especially on the ruffle around my neck. How could I have forgotten? The first time I clowned, I had powdered my face at each stage but had forgotten my neck. I thought I would never get the white greasepaint off my bright orange costume.

I ended up taking the make-up off in spots and patching it up the best I could. Not the best job in the world, but passable.

It was so much easier, though, after that. Now I never forget to set the greasepaint with powder at every step. It's part of the routine.

I find that reading God's Word regularly has that kind of effect on me spiritually. Like the powder, it sets God's principles in my life. It reminds me day by day of His faithfulness down through the centuries. And it renews and strengthens my faith when it is part of my routine.

PRAYER: Dear Lord, help me to make reading the Bible an integral part of my day and my life. Give me a new hunger for Your Word. I desire greater insight into the meaning of Scripture and how I may apply it to my daily life.

THE PARABLE OF
THE HATCHLESS EGGS

But whoso shall offend one of these little ones which believe in me, it were better for him that a millstone were hanged about his neck, and that he were drowned in the depth of the sea. Matthew 18:6

Mother honked the horn again. The sunlight was fading away on that chilly winter afternoon, and we had a couple of hours to drive to get home. "He'd better come on. We don't want to get home too late," Daddy said with an impatient edge to his usually calm voice.

We were waiting for my younger brother to emerge from the old, weather-beaten farmhouse where we had spent the day with relatives. Finally the door burst open and Bob fairly flew to the car on his short, four-year-old legs. My older brother opened the door behind the driver's seat in readiness. That was Bob's spot in the car. But to our surprise, he ran to the front door and insisted on riding in front by the window.

"Bobby, why don't you have your sweater on? You'll catch cold in this weather," Mother chided him.

"Oh, I had to keep the eggs warm," he explained, thrusting his carefully held bundle down in front of the car heater.

"The eggs?" Daddy asked.

"Yes, Daddy," he replied, wide-eyed with excitement. "They gave me two duck eggs and told me I'd have to be sure to keep them very warm so they would hatch out. I'm going to have some baby ducks!"

"That's nice," Mother said, "but are you warm enough?"

"Oh, yes," Bob insisted. "In fact, I'm kinda' hot."

All the way home, he leaned forward in an awkward position, keeping watch over his duck eggs. The warmth of the heater and the motion of the car almost lulled him to sleep. Our parents tried to get him to lean on Daddy and take a nap--but nothing could interrupt his vigil over the precious eggs.

When we finally got home, he insisted that he was still too hot to put on his sweater, and he kept the eggs carefully protected in its folds. Once inside, he complained that he was cold, so that Daddy would light the heater right away. He then knelt down in front of the fire, holding the eggs toward the flames.

It was all my parents could do to persuade him to go to bed. Mother got a box and carefully lined it with rags, explaining that she would make a warm nest for the eggs and cover them up. Finally, Daddy got the eggs out of Bob's clutches to place them in the box.

That's when Daddy discovered that the "duck eggs" were really small egg-shaped gourds. One of our relatives had played a joke on my brother. Just then, Bob asked excitedly, "Do you think they'll hatch out by morning? Won't it be great to have my own baby ducks?"

Daddy didn't have the heart to tell him it was a prank. So Bob went to bed with visions of ducklings running through his head. When he woke up the next morning, he darted to the box in anticipation. "They haven't hatched yet," he announced, "but I bet they will today."

Finally, our parents had to tell him the awful truth--that there weren't going to be any baby ducks from those "eggs." He was heartbroken as only a four-year-old can be, when his fondest hopes have been dashed. He had believed the teasing relative, only to be betrayed and bitterly disappointed. Although no harm was intended, the result was a traumatic experience for a trusting child.

How many times do our words or actions cause havoc and distress in the lives of others--sometimes without our even realizing their impact? We never know who is watching us as an example of what a Christian should be. Knowing that we are going to be held accountable for others we have injured and caused to stumble should provide a real incentive for us to weigh our words and actions.

PRAYER: Dear Lord, help me today to be a worthy example of a Christian. Guide me in all I say and do, so that I won't be a detriment to Your name and kingdom. May my words and deeds be pleasing in Your sight this day and every day.

THE PARABLE OF THE ENTHUSIASTIC STUDENTS

And they said one to another, Did not our heart burn within us, while he talked with us by the way, and while he opened to us the scriptures?   Luke 24:32

"Do we get out of school to go?" one of my seventh-grade music students asked with uncharacteristic enthusiasm.

"Yes," I replied. "It's in the morning. But I really don't think you should attend the concert if getting out of school is your only reason for wanting to go."

"That's enough reason for me," the reluctant scholar shot back with an ear-to-ear grin.

"Yeah," several others chimed in.

"It's worth a couple of bucks to get out of English and math," another one offered.

Before it was over, nearly every member of my very worst-behaved and least-interested music class had vowed to go to hear the student concert of the Dallas Symphony Orchestra. I was not overjoyed at the thought of taking this particular group of rough-and-tumble kids anywhere--especially to a concert. "They'll be a negative influence on the younger students," I thought.

133

This class had proved to be my greatest challenge in my first year at that particular school. As far as they were concerned, the word *music* meant rock'n'roll, with a little country music thrown in. Anything else was "really dumb."

"Well, they certainly are enthusiastic about going to the concert," I pondered. "Now all I have to do is get them to be that enthusiastic about what they're going to hear once they get there. But that's just about impossible."

I looked over the program again. One segment of the concert was going to be several excerpts from the opera *Carmen*.

I could imagine what their reaction would be if I even mentioned the word *opera* to them. "A bunch of dried-up old women screaming their heads off," one of them had defined the term earlier.

Knowing the day would be a complete disaster if I hadn't somehow whetted their interest and prepared them for the occasion, I doggedly decided to give it my best shot.

"Some of the music we're going to hear is about this really knockout of a chick," I started out, trying to use their language. Most of the boys, mature beyond their twelve to fourteen years of age as far as female pulchritude was concerned, pricked up their ears. I went on with the story, using their terminology and inserting some humor whenever possible. I acted out some of the story, even putting a plastic rose between my teeth.

They all seemed to find the setting of the bullfight rather exciting. Midway into the class, even the most indifferent students seemed interested.

"Now there's this song about the bullfight that Carmen liked to sing," I ventured tentatively. "Would you like to hear the words?"

"Yeah," most of them said.

I watched their faces as I tried to read the words as dramatically as possible.

"How does it go?" one of them asked, as if on cue.

I played part of it on the piano. "Would you like to try to sing it?" I asked, a little braver now.

"Yeah," they agreed.

Before the period was over, they were singing part of the chorus of the "Toreador Song" with gusto.

The next week I casually threw in the fact that *Carmen* is an opera.

"No kidding?" one of them said. They learned some of the other songs, and from then on, they wanted to sing "that opera" every time they came to class.

The trip to the youth concert was successful beyond my fondest hopes. My students behaved like ladies and gentlemen and seemed genuinely to enjoy the program. I was amazed. It took a lot of enthusiasm and energy to get them interested and excited, but it was worth the effort.

How much more worthwhile it is to share the good news of the Gospel and our Christian faith. Our enthusiasm for what God has done in our lives and our faithfulness in relating our experience and the experience of others to someone else's need can develop a thirst for the things of God. Most of all, being a conduit of God's love and grace can lead to a turning point in another's spiritual life.

PRAYER: Lord, give me enthusiasm and wisdom as I try to share Your love and redeeming power with others. Show me how to relate Your message to the lives and needs of those You bring into my life. Grant me drawing power, that my words may give others a hunger and a great desire for You.

THE PARABLE OF
THE UNFAIR PARKING TICKET

. . . Ye have not, because ye ask not.　　　　James 4:2

I couldn't believe my eyes! There was a parking ticket on my windshield. A closer look revealed that there also was a parking meter, its red flag proudly displayed, guarding the place I had chosen to park.

"That's not fair," I muttered to the wind. The parking meter had not been there when I had parked my car-- only a pole.

The city was in the process of changing the parking meters downtown. "I can't believe they put a new parking meter on while I was in the library, and then a policeman came by and gave me a ticket," I grumbled. It seemed like some sort of sinister plot to get my money.

"I may just go to court," I told my husband. "After all, I couldn't put money in a meter that wasn't even there."

"Why don't you call the Police Department and explain what happened?" he queried. "Maybe they'll just take care of it."

"Well, I guess it wouldn't hurt anything," I agreed. "I can think of other ways I'd rather spend $15."

After procrastinating for several days, I finally dialed the Traffic Division's number and soon found myself talking with a very personable police sergeant. I explained the situation. He chuckled and said, "Well, ma'am, I'll tell you what. You just put that ticket in an envelope with a little note saying what happened, and mail it to my attention. We'll just cancel that ticket out."

I was so glad I had asked. That was all I had to do. Instead of paying an unjust fine, we used the money to go out to eat after church the following Sunday.

God's Word tells us that we have not because we ask not. If a police sergeant is willing to listen to my tale of woe and make amends, how much more is my heavenly Father interested in my needs? All I have to do is ask.

I hadn't violated the law when I received the ticket, but even when I am guilty in God's eyes, He's always ready to forgive and "cancel my ticket." All I have to do is ask.

PRAYER: Dear Lord, I thank You that I can come to You with boldness in every situation, asking that my needs be met. I'm grateful that You never fail to meet those needs in the best way--even though at times I don't understand what's happening. Lord, help me to remember to ask, as You have directed.

THE PARABLE OF
THE UNFORTUNATE ACCIDENT

It is impossible but that offences will come: but woe unto him, through whom they come!   Luke 17:1

Instinctively I slammed on the brakes with all my might-- but it was too late. I had not seen the young boy on the bicycle until he was about four feet from my car. He had darted out from behind a parked truck and was going fast.

I heard the sickening thud as he crashed into the passenger side of my car. His bike sailed up in the air, landing on the curb. I could not see what had happened to him.

"Oh, dear God, please let him be alive!" I prayed as I tried desperately to get out of the car. I was so upset that, at first, I couldn't figure out why I was unable to move: I had on my seatbelt. It seemed like forever before I could control my fingers well enough to unfasten it.

Finally, I raced to the boy. At least he was still breathing. By this time, some neighbors had arrived, and one of them ran to call an ambulance.

I felt terrible! As they loaded the boy into the ambulance, I agonized, "Why did I have to drive down this particular street at that particular moment?" Even though he had run into me and there was nothing I could have done to avoid the accident, I was heartsick that I had played a part in his being injured. I would have done anything to change it, but it was too late. It had already happened. The result was the same, regardless of the intent.

Fortunately, the boy recovered and did not have permanent physical injury.

But I wonder-- How many times have my actions or my words caused injury to others, perhaps even without my knowing it? I may not mean to hurt someone else by thoughtless deeds or remarks, but the result will be the same, regardless of my intent.

PRAYER: Dear Lord, please help me to be ever mindful of the effect my words and actions have on others. Give me Your grace and wisdom to behave in a manner appropriate to the high calling You have given me as Your child. I don't want to be a stumbling block. Correct me when I unwittingly fall into error.

THE PARABLE OF
THE FASCINATING LIGHT

There is a way that seemeth right unto a man, but the end thereof are the ways of death.   Proverbs 16:25

Somehow a wasp had gotten into my office area. Armed with a fly swatter, I pursued the little rascal every time I heard his wings rustling behind the drapes or saw him flitting by out of the corner of my eye. This went on for some time, with the swift-winged creature successfully evading all my attempts to lay him to rest so that I could peacefully pursue my writing.

He was amazingly distracting as he raced around the room, sometimes seeming to dive-bomb my head in the midst of his flight.

Finally, I heard a loud buzzing. THe wasp was flailing around in the bottom of the light fixture, where he had been attracted by the bright lights. At one point, he managed to crawl to the edge and almost escaped. But a gentle nudge with the fly swatter returned him to his hot prison. He struggled feebly for a few more seconds and then lay lifeless. The fascinating light, which he had found so attractive and so magnetic, was the very thing that caused his death.

It's the same with sin and the wiles of satan. Often what appears to be exciting, adventurous, and alluring has the same effect on our spiritual lives as the light had on the wasp. It can lure us into a no-win, dead-end situation.

PRAYER: Dear Lord, guard me from the attraction of worldly pleasures that would be destructive in my life and detrimental to my walk with You. Help me to desire godly things and to be drawn to the path that You would have me walk in this earthly life.

THE PARABLE OF
THE STAINED-GLASS WINDOWS

And they that be wise shall shine as the brightness of the firmament; and they that turn many to righteousness as the stars for ever and ever. Daniel 12:3

What can compare with the breathtaking beauty of the majestic cathedrals of Europe? Hundreds of years old, they are magnificently ornamented by the loving hands of artists who dedicated their lives and talents to creating something exquisitely lovely to honor their God.

I entered each one with awe, sensing the lingering presence of the hundreds of thousands who had entered and worshiped there down through the ages. The architecture and style varied from cathedral to cathedral, but there was a common thread throughout: the stained-glass windows--so ethereally gorgeous that I found it difficult to breathe. The brilliant sunlight made the windows sparkle like crystal.

One of our visits, however, was during a thunderstorm. Even though it was early in the afternoon, the sky blackened, and darkness nearly enveloped us as we puddled our way to the cathedral's entrance. It was an unusually stately structure--one I had especially looked forward to seeing. But as I slipped inside, my spirit did not soar as it had in our other visits.

I looked around. It was indeed beautiful . . . but something seemed to be missing. And then it hit me. There was no sunlight streaming through the stained-glass windows. No doubt the artistry and workmanship were comparable to others we had seen. But the windows appeared dark and lifeless.

It was only after we left the cathedral and looked back that we could get some idea of their loveliness. Then we could see the light shining from within the church through the windows.

People are like stained-glass windows. They shine with brilliance in the sun. But when darkness comes, they continue to shine only if there is light inside. It's the glow from within that creates the beauty.

PRAYER: Lord, help me to shine with Your light at all times. When the dark times come--as they inevitably will--please enable me to continue to glow from within, resting in the assurance that Your competent and caring hands are working all things together for my good. I desire to be used to bring Your light and love into a dark and dying world.

THE PARABLE OF THE LOBSTER TRAP

Keep me from the snares which they have laid for me, and the gins of the workers of iniquity. Psalms 141:9

The restaurant was perched right on the Atlantic Ocean, overlooking the rugged coast of Maine. Just being there was delicacy enough, with the waves gently massaging the sand, the sailing vessels bobbing quaintly in the breeze, and the seagulls soaring in graceful flight. One paused, settling briefly on the windowsill. He cocked his head and looked our way as if bringing greetings from his airborne friends.

I had already decided I could not leave Maine without trying its trademark fare--lobster. I was tempted to get the lobster roll, since I had no idea how to begin to eat a whole lobster. Finally, however, all three of us decided to rise to the challenge and order whole lobsters. There the curious red-armored creatures sat, on our plates, seeming to stare at us with their glassy eyes. "What an imagination our Creator has," I thought as I examined the uniqueness of this creature from the deep.

We found the meat delicious and the experience hilarious as we tried to learn the right technique for cracking claws and fishing out the reward without spraying ourselves in the process.

Later we learned how the lobsters became our dinner instead of still enjoying their underwater crustacean life. They were lured into traps. Each bobbing buoy we saw as we drove along the coast in Acadia National Park signaled a lobster pot or creel set out by fishermen. All the lobster pots were color-coded and registered. Stealing another fisherman's lobsters is a serious offense.

The traps are built in two sections. The first part consists of a funnel-shaped opening. The lobster is enticed inside by bait of dead fish. After eating these morsels, the lobster notices more food through a second opening. Once inside the second chamber, he is faced with a blank wall and, because of his stiff skeleton, is unable to turn back around and escape.

"Well, at least they only have to look out for one kind of bait--dead fish," I mused. As Christians, we can be lured by many different kinds of snares in our path. They can even be things that are good but, when carried to extremes, can become gods in our lives as surely as carved idols. We need to be constantly aware of anything that would divert us from our purpose of worshiping and serving God wholeheartedly.

PRAYER: Dear Lord, I ask You this day to install a spiritual alarm system within me so that I may be warned when the enticements of this world would tempt me and entrap me. Give me Your wisdom and strength to recognize and to resist any influences that are contrary to Your will and Your way for my life.

THE PARABLE OF
THE FADED DRESS

Put on the whole armour of God, that ye may be able to stand against the wiles of the devil. For we wrestle not against flesh and blood, but against principalities, against powers, against the rulers of the darkness of this world, against spiritual wickedness in high places.

Ephesians 6:11-12

I was running late. I snatched one of my favorite "teaching" dresses out of the closet. "Better run an iron over it. It looks a little wrinkled," I thought as I tried to hurry.

I was almost through pressing the orchid print dress when I noticed the shoulders. "I can't wear this!" I said aloud. "The material on the shoulders is faded. How could that have happened?"

I quickly found a dress that did not need pressing, threw it on, and rushed out the door. On our way to school, I told my husband about the faded dress. "I won't be able to wear it anymore," I said. I liked to wear it to school; it was so comfortable. And the children loved it, especially with my orchid shoes. I was always amazed at the way young children noticed everything about me, down to the tiniest detail.

"I can't figure out how it got so faded," I told my husband, hoping he could come up with an answer. But he was as mystified as I was.

Later that day, I shared the puzzle with a friend. "You probably washed it and hung it out in the afternoon sun," she suggested.

"No," I replied, "I never line-dry it."

Even though I never wore the dress again, I couldn't bring myself to throw it away. But every time I saw it hanging in the closet, I would wonder, "How did it get that way?" The next time we went to Galveston, I discovered the answer.

Whenever we traveled, I always hung my clothes by the window behind the driver's seat. As we drove home on a hot summer afternoon, I noticed the sun beating down on my clothes on the west side of the car, and I realized that a couple of trips like that was all it had taken to fade my favorite dress.

Our joy as Christians is like that dress.

We can be so beautiful in our enthusiasm and dedication and then, seemingly overnight, discover that our joy has faded. We may not even know why our zeal just isn't as great as it was at first. It's not always easy to find the answer. Chances are, though, that we have allowed other things to fade our ardor for the things of God.

Satan is always eager to rob us of our joy. We have to be always watchful and not put ourselves in a position to be faded.

THE PARABLE OF
THE VALUABLE STONE

Verily, verily, I say unto you, He that believeth on me, the works that I do shall he do also; and greater works than these shall he do; because I go unto my Father. John 14:12

"HE PAID $10 FOR A STONE WORTH $2 MILLION," the newspaper headline proclaimed. The article told the fascinating story of a dramatic purchase that took place at the annual Gem and Mineral Show in Tucson, Arizona.

A gem dealer was looking around for something to buy for his two sons, who had pooled their money to give him $10 to buy them a rock. He noticed the blue-violet stone, the size of a potato, in the Tupperware bin of a gem dealer at the show. The prospective buyer picked it up, carefully looked it over, and then tried to keep his voice calm as he asked, "Do you want $15 for this?"

The seller, believing that his prospect thought the price too high, and realizing that the stone didn't look as pretty as the others in his $15 assortment, immediately lowered the price to $10. After all, he didn't want to lose a sale. The buyer tried to appear nonchalant as he handed over the $10--but once outside, he "let out a big holler." He knew he had something special.

Since then, the stone has been certified as a 1,905-carat natural star sapphire, about 800 carats heavier than the largest-known stone of this kind in the world. It has been appraised at $2.28 million. Money from the sale of the gem will be placed in a trust fund for the buyer's sons.

Unfortunately for the seller, he had no idea of the value of what was his.

How many times are we Christians like that man? We have inherited untold riches and have been entrusted with greater power than most of us will ever use or even suspect. We just don't understand the value of what we hold. Jesus told us that He would give us the authority and ability to do all the things He did during His earthly ministry--and more. If only we could get hold of and step out on that promise, nothing could stop the Christian church.

PRAYER: Dear Lord, I thank You for the rich inheritance that is mine. Help me to understand what I have been given. Give me Your wisdom in exercising the power and authority Jesus bought for me on the cross, and the boldness to step out in faith and use it for Your glory.

THE PARABLE OF
THE CONTRARY COMPUTER

We then that are strong ought to bear the infirmities of the weak, and not to please ourselves.   Romans 15:1

"No! I don't want to take a course in operating my computer!" I almost screeched. "I tell you the thing won't work!"

"Now, sometimes it's because we just don't understand how the computer operates," the condescending voice on the other end of the line droned on. "Our courses really aren't very expensive. I'm sure one could help you."

I hung up, my voice choked with tears of exasperation. "If one more person makes it sound like I'm just stupid and it's all my fault, I think I'll scream," I muttered through clenched teeth to the four walls.

I had purchased a high-powered computer and all the accompanying paraphernalia. I had looked forward to starting work immediately on a new book. However, the last several weeks had turned into one frustration after another. I could not get the thing to work!

The first computer had something wrong with it. They gave me a new one, but I couldn't get it to work either. Phone call after phone call brought increasing frustration. I couldn't find anyone in that huge company who would take the time to help solve my problem.

I felt like throwing the whole $6,000 investment in the trash!

Finally, I found a man who told me he would stick with me until we got the computer up and running. He had nothing to gain--made no commission except the satisfaction of helping someone get to the root of the problem.

His examination revealed that the first computer had damaged some of the software and that the graphics board--essential to the word-processing program--was defective.

Later, the Lord showed me the importance of being the kind of person in the spiritual lives of others who would hang in there until a problem was solved. Often we need help in understanding a certain principle or in getting past a particular spiritual problem. At those times, we need someone who will stick with us, someone who will invest time and godly wisdom in our lives, someone who will give us encouragement and show us the way.

We also need to be that "someone" to others.

PRAYER: Lord, I thank You for all those You have brought into my life who have invested their time and love in helping me to mature spiritually and to better know and understand Your ways and purpose in my life. I ask You this day to develop within me a real desire to help others in this same, beautiful way. Help me to be faithful and not to give up on one of Your children, just as You have never given up on me.

THE PARABLE OF
THE UNEXPECTED CHECK

I have been young, and now am old; yet have I not seen the righteous forsaken, nor his seed begging bread.

Psalms 37:25

Well, that was the last of the milk. With two toddlers and no money in the bank, that was not a very cheerful realization.

The last four years had not been easy financially. Going from two paychecks for two people to one paycheck for four proved to be a continuing challenge. But I felt that I should stay at home with my children instead of leaving them to be cared for by someone else.

This month, unexpected medical expenses had eaten into my meager grocery budget. Payday was two weeks away, and there was little in the cupboard; we had definitely run out of money before we ran out of month. "Mother Hubbard has nothing on us," I thought grimly.

The day before, I had talked with the Lord. "You know the need, Father," I had implored. "Please help us. I don't know how You'll do it, but I'm depending on You to provide food for the rest of the month."

As I said that prayer, faith welled up inside. But today, it seemed that my faith had been poured out with that last glass of milk.

I heard the postman's step on the porch and the click of the mailbox. I trudged out the door thinking, "There will probably be some new bills waiting for me."

To my surprise, there was a letter from a magazine to which I had submitted an article over a year ago. As I unfolded the letter, a piece of paper fell out onto the floor. Quickly I retrieved it and found that it was a check for fifty dollars. The letter explained that although the editor was unable to use my article, he was sending me the check because he had held it so long and had kept me from submitting it to another magazine. I had never had that happen before, nor has it happened since.

In the early 1960s, fifty dollars would buy a lot of groceries--enough for two weeks and then some. Talk about being blessed, excited, and more convinced than ever that God hears and answers prayer!

God always stands ready to hear and to answer our petitions. He sees our need even before we ask. We can depend on Him for the answer--even when it seems impossible.

PRAYER: Dear Lord, I give You praise and thanksgiving for meeting my every need. Thank You for Your provision in the past, this day, and forevermore. Help me to be anxious for nothing, knowing that, for the Creator of the whole universe, nothing is impossible.

THE PARABLE OF THE UNDISCOVERED LIGHT SWITCH

Therefore, my beloved brethren, be ye stedfast, unmoveable, always abounding in the work of the Lord, forasmuch as ye know that your labour is not in vain in the Lord.

1 Corinthians 15:58

It was our first night in our new home--new to us, that is. Actually the house was about twenty-five years old and was the house of our dreams. Exhausted from trying to get moved in, I was just crawling into bed when I remembered that I had not switched off the lights in the living room.

"Would you mind going to the living room and turning off the lights?" I hopefully asked my husband.

"Oh, okay," he sighed wearily.

He was back in a minute, his mission carried out--with one exception. He couldn't find the switch for a swag lamp that hung in the corner. It had been already turned on when we came in that morning. "I looked and looked," he explained. "I don't think it has a switch."

"Oh, men, anyway," I was muttering to myself as I crept down the hall. "They can look right at something and not see it."

I fully expected to find the light switch practically under the lamp, beside the French doors that led to the porch. No light switch there and none on the lamp itself. I looked on the other wall. Not there either. On the other side of the French doors. Nope. Around the corner in the dining room. Still no luck. "Well, I give up," I said irritably to the light fixture. "You can just burn all night for all I care."

The next morning I started a more thorough search for the elusive light switch. I looked out on the back porch, on the other side of the entrance into the dining room, beyond the large window near the French doors. Soon I enlisted the whole family in the search. All four of us looked everywhere we could think of. Still no light switch.

The diligent little lamp burned day and night for about two weeks. All the while I was insisting that surely there must be some way to turn it off.

One Saturday I was dusting the organ at the other end of the room. There, behind the drape that hung over sliding glass doors at least thirty feet from the lamp, was a light switch. "I wonder what that's for," I mused. A flip of the switch and the light went off.

At last, the mystery was solved. But I learned something from that lamp. "How wonderful," I thought, "to get so turned on to Jesus that no person or circumstance can possibly find and hit our 'off' switch. Then we would be as faithful as that hanging lamp that just burned and burned and burned, ever brightly."

PRAYER: Dear Lord, kindle my desire to serve You with a new intensity. I want to be Your light and shine brightly for You in every situation. Help me to avoid being governed by circumstances that would diminish my glow. Empower me to emit a consistently bright beacon of Your hope, concern, and love.

THE PARABLE OF
THE "SQUATTY" BREAD

How then shall they call on him in whom they have not believed? and how shall they believe in him of whom they have not heard? and how shall they hear without a preacher?   Romans 10:14

Every time we went to Galveston, the kids would always say during the drive, "I hope Grandma made us some 'Grandma's bread.'" Long before we got to her house, we could almost smell that enticing, magical aroma of freshly baked Italian bread and taste that first delicious bite.

Grandma never disappointed us. It was always there, waiting for us. And she never tired of hearing our *oohs* and *ahs* about how good it was.

I decided to learn how to make "Grandma's bread." I had watched her before, and it didn't look too hard-- even though there was a lot of kneading over a period of several hours. I asked her for her recipe, but she didn't have anything written down. "Oh, just a pinch of this and a little bit of that," was about all she could tell me. Not too precise for a novice bread baker.

I went home, all charged up and ready to make those first wonderful loaves of "Grandma's bread." Everyone was so excited. "My mama's going to make us some 'Grandma's bread,' the children proudly told all the neighborhood kids.

I carefully mixed the ingredients according to my sketchy recipe and covered the dough with a towel to let it rise. The morning was dotted with periodic trips to the kitchen to knead the dough. "This is fun," I thought-- "really therapeutic." Smashing that dough was an ideal way to get rid of frustrations. Finally, I let the dough rise for the final time and popped the pans into the oven.

My kitchen smelled just like Grandma's. Little visitors kept dropping in, wanting to know when the bread was going to emerge from the oven. Finally, the time was up. But to my disappointment, the bread did not look like "Grandma's bread" at all. It had not risen to the same glorious heights.

Oh, it smelled the same and it had the same flavor. But it was not fluffy and light like Grandma's.

On our next visit, I tried to figure out where I had gone wrong. I questioned her in detail. I had my husband listen too, since he understood her thick Italian accent better than I. She went through the process step by step. No clue there.

I tried several times to make the bread. My family always encouraged me, and it didn't taste bad. It was just that it wasn't like "Grandma's bread." In fact, I felt like naming it "squatty bread" because it never did rise the way it was supposed to.

Then one day, in the food section of the newspaper, I spotted an article on bread-making. It said that one of the secrets is to have the water just the right temperature. If it's too hot, the article explained, the water will hinder the yeast's work of making the bread rise. "That's it!" I shouted. "My idea and Grandma's idea of 'warm' weren't the same. The water I used was too hot."

The next time I made "Grandma's bread," it was more like Grandma made it . . . never quite the same, but almost. At least it lost its name of "squatty bread" that very day.

Sharing Jesus with others is like making "Grandma's bread." It takes time--in some cases, a lot of time. You have to keep working with a person--"kneading the dough." You also have to use wisdom in choosing your approach. If you come on too strong--if your words are too "hot"--you may turn someone off instead of on to the gospel message. It takes time, patience, and love. But the end result--just as in making "Grandma's bread"--is worth it all.

PRAYER: Dear Lord, give me Your wisdom when I try to share the good news of salvation. Help me to be patient and loving as I develop trusting relationships with others so that they will be willing to listen to my words. Thank You for those You bring into my life for Your guidance.

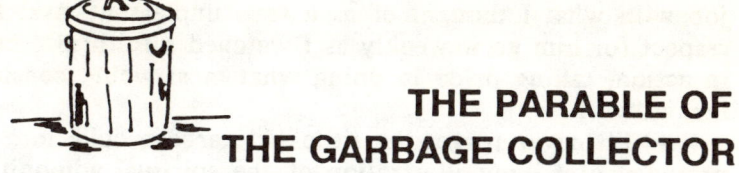

THE PARABLE OF
THE GARBAGE COLLECTOR

And he said unto him, Well, thou good servant: because thou hast been faithful in a very little, have thou authority over ten cities.   Luke 19:17

"Lady!" I heard a shrill voice say between bangs on the kitchen door. "Lady!"

"Who on earth could that be?" I thought with some irritation. We had moved into our first home only weeks before, and I was trying to feed my brand-new infant son.

"Lady!" he called persistently.

"Just a minute!" I shouted. "I'm coming!"

I opened the door and almost closed it again. There stood a wizened little old man. His lower eyelids bagged down, exposing redness beneath his bloodshot eyes.

"Lady," he said, holding up a rickety old lamp, "I pick up your trash and I just wanted to be sure you hadn't put this out by mistake. It seemed too good to throw away."

"No, I don't want it anymore," I replied.

"I just wanted to be sure," he explained. "I sure didn't want to haul off something you valued."

By now I had gotten used to his somewhat unusual appearance. "It was very thoughtful of you to take the trouble to ask," I told him sincerely.

"Well, I try to do a good job," he said, beaming with pride. "Now you just let me know if I'm not doing something to please you."

We lived outside the city limits and paid a monthly fee to have our garbage collected each week. The old man came inside the garage to collect it, saving me from having to put it out on the street. I had noted, too, that he always lined the garbage can with fresh newspapers once he had emptied its content. "Very unusual," I reflected. "Nice."

I started looking forward to seeing the little old man. He was a quaint sight, driving his battered truck as if he were an army general on his way to complete a mission of great importance. He took such pains to do an excellent job with what I thought of as a very unpleasant task. My respect for him grew weekly as I watched a faithful person in action, taking pride in doing what most would consider menial work.

I'll never forget the little old garbage collector. He provided a striking illustration of the spiritual admonition found in Ecclesiastes 9:10: "Whatsoever thy hand findeth to do, do it with thy might."

Whenever I'm given a lowly task to do, I recall his example of faithfulness, knowing that if we are faithful in little things, God will trust us with greater things to do for Him.

PRAYER: Lord, I want to be a faithful servant. Help me to remember that there are no small tasks in Your kingdom. Give me a heart to do my very best in each thing You give my hands to do, for I know that You look for constancy as a qualification for greater responsibility.

THE PARABLE OF
THE UNASSEMBLED FIRE TRUCK

And we beseech you, brethren, to know them which labour among you, and are over you in the Lord, and admonish you; and to esteem them very highly in love for their work's sake. I Thessalonians 5:12-13

With keen anticipation, my husband and I pictured our three-year-old racing around in the shiny red fire engine we had bought him for Christmas. It was just the kind of toy he would like and was just right for his stage of development.

We decided not to assemble it until we got to my parents' home for the Christmas holidays. After all, it couldn't be too difficult to put together, and it was easier to protect it from Rick's eyes if we kept it in the box, carefully wrapped in brown paper.

Christmas Eve was surrounded by an air of excitement. It was harder than usual to get Rick and his sister, Laurie, settled down for the evening and, finally, asleep. We then went into the living room with the secret package and opened it for the first time. There were quite a few more parts than we had anticipated, but the "easy-to-follow" directions were included. "This shouldn't take long," my husband said confidently.

Before it was over, we decided that the directions should have included a warning: "Degree in engineering necessary." The assembly proved to be a much more challenging task than we had ever imagined, and it took us most of the night to finish it. The results, though, were great. Carefully closing the living-room door on the appealing toy we had labored over, we sleepily went to bed. About two hours later, Rick jumped on top of our bed, eager to see what he would get for Christmas. Finally he got everyone up, and we went into the living room. His eyes grew as big as saucers when he saw the red fire engine sitting under the Christmas tree. His excitement and delight made all the effort of the night before seem worthwhile, as we watched him get into the fire truck and pedal away, making appropriate sound effects as he went.

Who would have dreamed that assembling a toy would be so complicated and take so much work? It looked so easy!

That's also true when we hear a sermon, lesson, or presentation that's well prepared and delivered. It looks so easy. And yet it probably took the speaker hours of study and preparation to get ready for the half-hour or so of presenting the material, specifically geared to that particular group. Being thoughtful enough to express our appreciation for that effort or to tell the speaker how the presentation helped in a certain situation can make that faithful person feel that his or her efforts were worthwhile.

PRAYER: Dear Lord, remind me to express my appreciation for those who labor in Your vineyard as preachers and teachers. Help me not to take for granted the tremendous effort that they put forth. Enable me to be a blessing and an inspiration to them, even as they are to me.

THE PARABLE OF
THE DARKENED ROOM

Then spake Jesus again unto them, saying, I am the light of the world: he that followeth me shall not walk in darkness, but shall have the light of life.   John 8:12

"Are you sure there will be enough light for us to see our music?" my friend and I asked the artist.

"Oh, yes," he assured us. "There will be plenty of light from the projector even after the lights dim."

We had agreed to play and sing as part of a chalk-talk presentation for Easter. We were to perform several pieces as the artist developed his drawings. The climax was at the end, when black light would be used to illuminate the glowing picture.

My friend hadn't memorized the words to the final song, and I couldn't play without the music, so we felt a little apprehensive. Since the audience was already arriving, we couldn't check out the light situation without ruining the element of surprise. "Well, the artist ought to know," I thought as we began the program.

Everything was going very well. We started on the last song. About midway through the piece, the lights began to dim. As the room grew darker and darker, my nose got closer and closer to the music. I glanced at Jeanette and saw, in the dim light, sheer panic in her eyes. Finally the room was almost pitch-black. It was true there was light from the projector--but it was way at the other end of the long room.

Someway, somehow I kept on playing and Jeanette kept on singing. Her words were original, to say the least, and the composer probably would have been hard put to recognize the accompaniment--but we finally got through the selection without total disaster.

Fortunately, we had played and sung enough in the past and were familiar enough with the piece to keep on going in the darkness.

Our Christian walk is like that too. If we learn the principles of God's Word and consistently practice those principles in good times, we will automatically follow them in hours of darkness. When we look to the "Light of the world" for illumination, we do not have to fear the blackest night.

PRAYER: Dear Lord, I give thanks for the gift of Your Son and the light He provides for the world and for my life. Give me a greater desire to live Your principles more consistently, so that I never have to fear the darkness. Thank You for illuminating my steps, one by one, as I attempt to walk in the way You have chosen for me.

THE PARABLE OF
THE DISCORDANT ORGAN

Jesus Christ the same yesterday, and to day, and for ever.
Hebrews 13:8

Several people were looking askance over their shoulders. The minister was peering over his spectacles. Seated at the small organ at the back of the tiny mission church we were attending, I was the object of their gaze. Their stares were greeted by an expression which must have registered utter bewilderment emanating from a face red with embarrassment.

The noise coming out of that organ was horribly discordant. It sounded like I was making a mistake at every other note. I stared in disbelief at my hands. Yes, they were playing the right notes. But the results jarred my ears.

We were singing "Faith of Our Fathers," a hymn I had probably played hundreds of times before . . . correctly. I was mystified and disconcerted at what was happening. The unkind glances in my direction increased. I unceremoniously ended the hymn after the second verse instead of singing all the verses. I thought, "I hope our forefathers' faith was better than that hymn sounded," as I nervously awaited the time to play the second hymn.

To my enormous relief, the second hymn sounded fine. Unfortunately, that was not the case during the offertory. Once more, the sound that issued forth from that instrument lied about the notes my fingers were playing. It was terrible! Fortunately, it didn't take long to collect the offering, since there were few people present on that cold, blustery winter day.

Mysteriously, the last hymn again was fine. At least the service *ended* on a harmonious note. Needless to say, I skipped the postlude. I wasn't going to push my luck, and I just wasn't up to any more merciless looks in my direction.

After the service, I started playing music detective to try to find out what on earth had happened. Finally, I discovered that all of the B-flats on the organ were playing the sound of B. Since the first hymn and the offertory were in flat keys, there had been a lot of clashing notes. At least I felt vindicated as a musician, but it didn't solve the problem, which continued periodically throughout the winter months.

It seemed that, when the weather was very cold and damp, the breezes penetrating the drafty old building had this strange effect on the organ. An organ technician could not come up with a solution either. Of course, the instrument would not perform in its perverted way when the repairman was present.

I always checked, before each service, to see if the B-flats were sounding accurately. But it was totally unpredictable. Sometimes, right in the middle of a hymn, it would begin its erratic behavior.

I had never noticed before how many hymns were written in flats. I would try to switch to another key, but even that didn't solve the problem when there were accidentals or a logical key happened to have an A-sharp. Have you ever tried to play something and remember not to hit a B-flat or an A-sharp?

I thought back to the story I had heard of the old master musician who, when asked, "What's the good word for today?" hit his tuning fork and replied, "The good news is that that sound is an A. It will always be an A, regardless of how much everything else may change."

"He obviously never had to try to play that wretched organ," I thought to myself.

Everything made by human hands is, at some point, unreliable. Scientific findings may be displaced by later findings or proven false. The things that can be counted on seem to be growing fewer every day. That's why it's so exciting in the midst of a changing world, replete with uncertainties and often confusing circumstances, to know that God--the Father, the Son, and the Holy Spirit--never changes, and that His Word and promises can be depended upon to be true, practical, and fruitful in our daily lives.

PRAYER: Dear Lord, I thank You that I can count on Your love, Your power, and Your faithfulness without reservation. I want You to be able to depend on me also. Please help me to be more and more consistent in my walk with You day by day.

THE PARABLE OF
THE MIMOSA SEEDLINGS

Be sober, be vigilant; because your adversary the devil, as a roaring lion, walketh about, seeking whom he may devour.
1 Peter 5:8

157

The spring had been an unusually wet, stormy one for this part of the country. Few days had missed at least an afternoon shower. Many times there had been drenching rains, resulting in severe flooding in the area.

Apparently this made the ground especially receptive to the sprouting of seedlings. The two mimosa trees in our backyard had also been unusually prolific in their production of seeds.

Every day, when I went out to admire with anticipation the growth of the plants in my flower beds, I found several of the pesky little mimosa sprouts pushing their way up through the soil. I swiftly plucked out the interlopers, realizing that the fast-growing trees would otherwise take firm root where they were not wanted.

A couple of years ago, one got an unnoticed head start in a bed tucked behind the house in a rather obscure spot. When I discovered the hearty-looking plant, it was sturdily and stubbornly rooted. I couldn't budge it by pulling or even by spading. Its long, strong roots remained unrelentingly in place. The only thing I can do is keep it hacked down to a nub. I sure don't want a tree growing that close to the house.

The mimosa seedlings are like the unwanted seeds that can be so easily sown in our lives if we're not watchful. Seeds of unforgiveness, resentment, unrighteousness, jealousy, unbelief are always seeking a place to grow. We can't let down our guard for even a moment. Otherwise, a tiny seed will take root and soon become a huge, overwhelming plant that can choke our peace, joy and love, and hamper our Christian walk.

This is especially true in the storms of life, when conditions seem unusually favorable for unwanted seedlings to grow.

PRAYER: Dear Lord, help me to plant seeds of right attitudes and purpose in my life this day. Guard me from unrighteous and un-Christlike thoughts and reactions. When one slips in, nudge me quickly so that I may uproot it promptly and not allow it to grow in my heart.

THE PARABLE OF
THE FADING SWEATER

And the ransomed of the Lord shall return, and come to Zion with songs and everlasting joy upon their heads: they shall obtain joy and gladness, and sorrow and sighing shall flee away.   Isaiah 35:10

"What a beautiful sweater!"

The first time I wore the lovely black and turquoise sweater I had bought in New York City, I received several compliments on it. I had considered it a real shopping find--most unusual, with a black orchid outlined in turquoise stitching on the front. And it was such a reasonable price. "Why, it would have cost twice that much at home," I had decided.

I felt very elegant in it--especially after the compliments--until I got home. Then, as I started to dress for bed, I noticed that the skin underneath my right arm was turquoise. A closer inspection revealed that part of my slip had also turned turquoise. Somehow the color just didn't do as much for the slip and for my skin as it did for the sweater.

The next morning I doused the sweater in cold soapy water, hoping not to ruin it. The water immediately took on a turquoise hue. Fortunately, the black did not fade. I soaked the sweater most of the day, running it through a number of rinse waters. It continued to fade, but a little less each time. After drying it, I found that it still looked all right, although the color isn't quite as vibrant.

This experience gave me a greater appreciation for the usually colorfast items that are made in our country. It's wonderful to be able to wash fabrics over and over, knowing that they will not fade.

It's the same with the joy that God gives us. It does not fade with circumstances. Regardless of what we might be going through, we can continue to have the joy of the Lord. Happiness comes and goes with the conditions that surround us. Ah, but joy! It's always present. It's fade-proof.

PRAYER: Dear Lord, I thank You for giving me Your joy that does not depend on what's happening around me. Help me to realize what a precious gift this is and to treasure it carefully.

THE PARABLE OF
THE ORIENTAL TERMITES

Take us the foxes, the little foxes, that spoil the vines; for our vines have tender grapes.   Song of Solomon 2:15

It was late afternoon as I walked into the dimly lit living room. Suddenly I noticed dozens of tiny pinpoints of daylight piercing the otherwise opaque draperies. "What on earth?" I thought as I raced to the window for a closer look. Sure enough, there were many, many small holes in the drapery fabric.

I called my husband. He was as puzzled as I was. What on earth could have caused this riddling of the material? We opened the drapes and found the answer. There, apparently drawn by the outside light, were a multitude of tiny-winged creatures. They looked something like ants, except for their delicate flying apparatus.

The next morning we called an exterminator. The man minutely inspected the little creatures, scratched his head, and said with a puzzled look, "They don't look like any termite I've ever seen, but I guess that's what they are. I've seen millions of the things, but these are different." He sprayed, then collected a specimen to send off for identification.

When the report came in, he called us. "They were termites all right," he reported, "but it's a type that's found only in the Orient. They're not Texas termites, so I don't have any idea how they got in your living room."

160

Their presence remained a mystery--until the day I went into the living room and found a couple of insects on the beautiful piece of driftwood we had made into a decorative tree. A closer look revealed a termite crawling out from inside one of the branches. My husband had bought the driftwood in a gift shop in Galveston about three years before.

With the help of the exterminator, we pieced together what must have happened. The driftwood was from somewhere in the Orient. The termite eggs, laid inside the wood years earlier, had remained dormant until they hatched in our living room. The tiny pests cost us new draperies and several weeks of puzzlement. And to think the eggs had been in our living room all that time!

All of us have hidden hurts . . . sometimes long-forgotten memories . . . that dwell within us. They linger in the deep recesses of our minds--sometimes so deeply buried that we don't even consciously recall them. But they're there nevertheless, just waiting to emerge and to cause destruction and pain to us and to others close to us.

The good news is that Jesus stands ready to exterminate these destructive spiritual termites and to repair the damage with His unconditional love.

PRAYER: Dear Lord, I thank You for Your healing power and that You are always ready to mend damaged spirits and to restore the years the locusts have eaten. Bring to my mind those past hurts and disappointments that continue to retard my spiritual growth. I thank You for applying Your healing balm and making me whole in every area.

THE PARABLE OF THE SPECTACULAR RAINBOW

For I am persuaded, that neither death, nor life, nor angels, nor principalities, nor powers, nor things present, nor things to come, nor height, nor depth, nor any other creature, shall be able to separate us from the love of God, which is in Christ Jesus our Lord. Romans 8:38-39

We rounded the curve, and there it was--the most gorgeous rainbow I had ever seen. The rain had been pouring as we drove over the flat, sandy Arizona countryside. In fact, we almost had to stop because of the deluge cascading down our windshield.

But all of a sudden, as if on cue, the rain ended, and the sun beamed out from behind the dark clouds. So began a spectacular light show that nature staged seemingly just for us. The startlingly beautiful hues of sunset intensified as the sun began to call it a day. The silhouettes of the tall, stately saguaro cacti, their arms upstretched toward heaven, added further drama to the scene. And now the rainbow, its colors brighter and more beautiful than any I remembered.

I caught my breath. It was almost too beautiful to endure. A feeling of awe and overwhelming respect for the Artist who created this magnificent scene swept over me. We had to stop now . . . to drink in this unique moment, to savor a spectacle such as we would probably never see again.

You see, rainbows are not always there to enjoy. Conditions have to be just right. For a rainbow to be visible, the sun, the eye of the observer, and the shower must all be in a straight line, with the sun behind the person.

Sometimes when things seem dark, and discouragement comes, when we're in the midst of a storm, it's hard to remember that the light is still there. But it *is* still there--even though it may be behind you rather than in full view. And, of course, it's often in those times that you learn the most and grow the most--the times when your rainbow can appear.

PRAYER: Lord, I thank You that nothing in this world nor any satanic force can separate me from Your love and power. Help me to remember always that, even when I don't feel Your presence, You are ever with me in every situation. Also, remind me that it is often in the darkest hours that Your glory is made manifest and that You shine through the rain to create a rainbow.

THE PARABLE OF
THE AIRLINE PILOT

Know therefore that the Lord thy God, he is God, the faithful God, which keepeth covenant and mercy with them that love him and keep his commandments to a thousand generations.   Deuteronomy 7:9

"I'm Captain James Matthews," the handsome, greying man said, extending his hand. "I'm your pilot for your flight to Jamaica. I just wanted to come back and say hello and let you know we're doing everything possible to make your flight safe and enjoyable. Oh, by the way, the copilot's in the cockpit and has everything under control," he said with a chuckle.

"What a pleasant surprise," I thought. That was the first time on any flight that I had seen the pilot of a plane until after it had landed and the passengers were disembarking. There was a ripple of excitement and good will as he made his way through the cabin of the plane. Everyone was pleased to meet the pilot face to face, and have a moment to chat with him.

I settled back to enjoy the flight. I had never been afraid of flying, but somehow I felt even more confident this time. After all, I had met the pilot, and I was convinced we were in good hands.

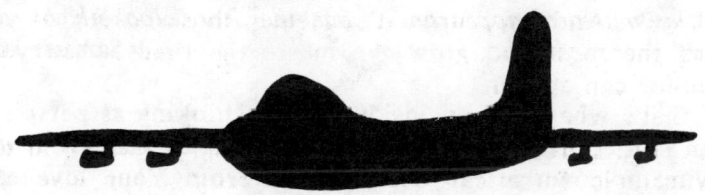

"Our spiritual journeys are like that too," I mused. God reveals Himself to us periodically in such a personal way that we almost feel as though He has reached down and shaken our hand. Once we have made Him the pilot of our lives and placed the controls in His hands, we can rest in the assurance that He has everything under control.

And, even when we don't understand what's happening and it looks like we're going to crash, we can still know that we're in capable, loving hands. After all, we've met the Pilot, and He has promised that He is working all things for our good (Romans 8:28).

PRAYER: Lord, I thank You that You are the Pilot of my life and that You do have everything under control. Help me to rest in that assurance, being anxious for nothing, with absolute confidence that You are ordering my steps and shaping my future with purpose.

THE PARABLE OF
THE CATHETERIZED HEART

. . . for the Lord seeth not as man seeth; for man looketh on the outward appearance, but the Lord looketh on the heart.   1 Samuel 16:7

"So that's what goes on inside," I was thinking as perspiration poured from my forehead. It was as though I was having my own private television screening, and my heart was playing the starring role.

The cold metal table, the awkward position, and the unbelievably hot dye that had been inserted into a main artery hardly combined for ideal viewing conditions. I felt as though I had suddenly been thrust into the middle of the Sahara Desert at high noon.

Classic symptoms of a heart attack had brought me here. The last few days had been filled with stress tests, electrodes plastered on my chest, heart monitors, and all kinds of x-rays. Suddenly that small, reliably performing organ that I had always taken for granted had become the controlling force in my very existence.

But this test--cardiac catheterization--certainly topped all the others. Instead of taking just x-rays, the doctors and technicians videotape the movement of the dye through the body.

This process enables them to check the function of the heart, the opening and closing of the heart valves, and the passage of the fluid through the arteries. Since the patient has to be awake when the test is run, he or she can watch the whole process along with the doctor.

"Well, I might as well enjoy this as much as possible," I mused uncomfortably. It was interesting to watch my own heart in action and to gain a glimmer of understanding of the vital role it plays and the work it must do. I was amazed at all that was going on.

Fortunately, the results of the test were reassuring. For me, it was a learning experience, one I will not soon forget.

We take so much for granted--even life itself. We take God for granted, and those He has brought into our lives. Too often we fail to be grateful for our numerous blessings.

We also tend to look at surface appearances, not really knowing--or caring--what is happening underneath. How often would we recognize an apparent weakness in another as heroic courage, if we only knew and understood what he is facing?

One thing is sure. Doctors can observe the function of a heart through the amazing use of technology, but only God can see and really know our "hearts."

PRAYER: Lord, thank You for health. Help me not to take this tremendous blessing for granted. I realize how important it is for my physical heart to function perfectly, but I also want to have a perfect heart, spiritually speaking. Show me what I must do for my heart to be pleasing in Your sight.

THE PARABLE OF
THE MANUFACTURER'S HANDBOOK

Thy word is a lamp unto my feet, and a light unto my path.
Psalms 119:105

Talk about excited! Our two preschoolers had waited for this moment since the day they overheard me phoning an order for a swing set. Now they were dancing around even before the truck driver unloaded their treasure.

The only problem was that, while they had visions of immediately swinging and going down the slide, the set arrived in hundreds of pieces that had to be put together. At least, we thought that was the only problem.

What we didn't know, as we carefully sorted out the parts and started the mammoth assembly job, was that the instructions we received were for a different set, not for the one that was delivered.

We would read, "Connect part X to part Y." Unfortunately, there was no part X or part Y in that set. The pieces just wouldn't fit together according to the diagram.

What a mess! We spent days figuring out how to put the pieces together by guesswork, bombarded by the unrelenting question: "When are we going to be able to swing?" Finally, we had it finished--with a couple of small parts left over. How much better and easier it would have been if we had had the right directions.

I like to think of the Bible as the Manufacturer's handbook for our lives. After all, God created us and He's the only one who knows how our lives should be put together and how they will work most effectively. Following the world's manual will lead to frustration and emptiness and, eventually, to destruction.

Want to live a successful, fulfilling, and eternally rewarding life? Then follow your Creator's directions.

PRAYER: Dear Lord, I recognize that You made me and You know everything about me as well as Your reason for creating me. You and only You know the exact role You want me to play in Your kingdom here on earth. Help me to follow Your direction and leading in every facet of my life. Show me how to develop and to use the abilities You have given me, and I'll give You all the glory.

LIST OF PARABLES BY TITLE

The Unexpected Check	Psalms 37:25	God's Provision	146
The Unexplained Desert	Isa 40:8	God's Faithfulness	19
The Unfair Parking Ticket	James 4:2	Prayer	135
The Unfortunate Accident	Luke 17:1	Impact on Others	137
The Unfruitful Tomato Plants	John 15:16	Bearing Fruit	45
The Unprepared Play	Phil 1:6	Talents	88
The Unseen Computer Codes	John 16:13	Holy Spirit	92
The Unwelcome Visitor	Matt 25:44-45	Ministering to Others	37
The Valuable Stone	John 14:12	Power of Believer	143
The Vanishing Footprints	2 Cor 4:7	Everlasting Results	80
The Volcanic Cake	James 3:17	Spiritual Principles	16
The Vulture	James 4:7	satan's Nature	125
The Wilted Zinnias	Gal 6:1-2	Ministering to Others	50
The Wrong Target	Matt 23:27-28	Outward Appearance	120
The Wrong-Way Dress	Isa 50:4	Counsel	121
The Yellow Jackets	Luke 11:24-26	satan's Persistence	33
The Young Opera Fans	Prov 22:6	Training Children	82

There are 37 Old Testament Scriptures and 64 New Testament Scriptures

LIST OF PARABLES BY SUBJECT

SUBJECT	TITLE	SCRIPTURE	PAGE
Appreciation	Unassembled Fire Truck	1 Thess 5:12-13	152
Bearing Fruit	Unfruitful Tomato Plants	John 15:16	45
Child of God	Sheep and Goats	Matt 25:33-34,41	15
Commitment	Catacombs	Phil 1:20-21	61
Commitment	Meticulous Paleontologists	Rom 2:7	101
Consistency	Undiscovered Light Switch	1 Cor 15:58	147
Commitment of Work/Speech Idea		Prov 16:3	63
Counsel	Puzzling Chickens	Prov 15:22	115
Counsel	Wrong-Way Dress	Isa 50:4	121
Dependence on God/Changed Student		Isa 50:7	103
Determination	Spunky Sparrows	2 Tim 4:7-8	98
Diligence	Minor Key	2 Pet 3:14	123
Direction	Misleading Signs	Isa 30:21	11
Discernment	Destructive Moths	2 Cor 11:13-14	23
Discipline	Undisciplined Fingers	Matt 26:41	59
Earthly Treasures	Starving Egrets	Psalms 31:19	118
Everlasting Results/Vanishing Footprints		2 Cor 4:7	80
Example	Baby Duckling	Titus 2:7	26
Example	Beautiful Rosebud	Rom 14:13	60
Faith	Overcast Day	2 Cor 5:7 Heb 11:6	95

PARABLES IN SCRIPTURE ORDER

For a free catalog of other books and magazines
lifting up the Light of the world,
send self-addressed, stamped envelope to

Star Books, Inc.
408 Pearson Street
Wilson, NC 27893

(919) 237-1591